Most Layers Are Liars

The Truth About Running A Small Business

Written By:

The Money Guy and The Tax Guy

Most Lawyers Are Liars - The Truth about Running A Small Business

You have a small business, now what? Well time to understand how this business works. Well, at lease how business within itself works. We will give you some tools that you can use, follow, and grow on. Remember nothing is set in stone, and never leave a stone unturned when running a small business.

You need organization and a proper plan

To succeed in business today, you need to be flexible and have good planning and organizational skills. Many people start a business thinking that they will turn on their computers or open their doors and start making money, only to find that making money in a business is much more difficult than they thought.

You can avoid this in your business ventures by taking your time and planning out all the necessary steps you need to achieve success. Whatever type of business you want to start, using the following nine tips can help you be successful in your venture.

Key Takeaways

- Starting a business requires analytical thinking, determined organization, and detailed record-keeping.

- It is important to be aware of your competition and either appropriate or improve upon their successful tactics.

- You will certainly end up working harder for yourself than you would for someone else, so prepare to make sacrifices in your personal life when establishing your business.

- Providing good service to your customers is crucial to gaining their loyalty and retaining their business.

9 Tips for Growing A Successful Business

1. Get Organized

To achieve business success, you need to be organized. It will help your complete tasks and stay on top of things to be done. An effective way to be organized is to create a to-do list each day. As you complete each item, check it off your list. This will ensure that you are not forgetting anything and completing all the tasks that are essential to the survival of your business.

2. Keep Detailed Records

All successful businesses keep detailed records. By doing so, you will know where the business stands financially and what potential challenges you could be facing. Just knowing this gives you time to create strategies to overcome those challenges.

3. Analyze Your Competition

Competition breeds the best results. To be successful, you cannot be afraid to study and learn from your competitors. They may be doing something right that you can implement in your business to make more money.

4. Understand the Risks and Rewards

The key to being successful is taking calculated risks to help your business grow. A good question to ask is "What's the downside?" If you can answer this question, then you know what the worst-case scenario is. This knowledge will allow you to take the kinds of calculated risks that can generate tremendous rewards.

Understanding risks and rewards includes being smart about the timing of starting your business. For example, did the severe economic dislocation of 2020 provide you with an opportunity (say, manufacturing and selling face masks) or an impediment (opening a new restaurant during a time of social distancing and limited seating allowed)?

5. Be Creative

Always be looking for ways to improve your business and make it stand out from the competition. Recognize that you do not know everything and be open to innovative ideas and different approaches to your business.

6. Stay Focused

The old saying "Rome wasn't built in a day" applies here. Just because you open a business does not mean you are going to immediately start making money. It takes time to let people know who you are, so stay focused on achieving your short-term goals.

7. Prepare to Make Sacrifices

The lead-up to starting a business is challenging work, but after you open your doors, your work has just begun. In many cases you must put in more time than you would if you were working for someone else, which may mean spending less time with family and friends to be successful.

8. Provide Great Service

There are many successful businesses that forget that providing great customer service is important. If you provide better service for your customers, they will be more inclined to come to you the next time they need something instead of going to your competition.

9. Be Consistent

Consistency is a key component to making money in business. You must keep doing what is necessary to be successful day in and day out. This will create long-term positive habits that will help you make money overall.

The Bottom Line

According to 2019 data from the U.S. Bureau of Labor Statistics, 20% of new businesses fail during the first two years of being open, 45% during the first five years, and 65% during the first 10 years. Only 25% of new businesses make it to 15 years or more. If you want to be among that 25%, rigorous attention to these nine tips is the smart way to get there.

The Basics of Financing a Business

There are a number of ways you can do it, each with its own plusses and minuses

What Is Business Financing?

Unless your business has the balance sheet of Apple, eventually you will need access to capital through business financing. In fact, even many large-cap companies routinely seek capital infusions to meet short-term obligations. For small businesses, finding the right funding model is vitally important. Take money from the wrong source and you may lose part of your company or find yourself locked into repayment terms that impair your growth for many years into the future.

Key Takeaways

- There are a number of ways to find financing for a small business.

- Debt financing is usually offered by a financial institution and is like taking out a mortgage or an automobile loan, requiring regular monthly payments until the debt is paid off.

- In equity financing, either a firm or an individual makes an investment in your business, meaning you do not have to pay the money back, but the investor now owns a percentage of your business, even a controlling one.

- Mezzanine capital combines elements of debt and equity financing, with the lender usually having an option to convert unpaid debt into ownership in the company.

What Is Debt Financing?

Debt financing for your business is something you understand better than you think. Do you have a mortgage or an automobile loan? Both are forms of debt financing. It works the same way for your business. Debt financing comes from a bank or some other lending institution. Although it is possible for private investors to offer it to you, this is not the norm.

Here is how it works. When you decide you need a loan, you head to the bank and complete an application. If your business is in the earliest stages of development, the bank will check your personal credit.

For businesses that have a more complicated corporate structure or have been in existence for an extended period time, banks will check other sources. One of the most important is the Dun & Bradstreet (D&B) file. D&B is the best-known company for compiling a credit history on businesses. Along with your business credit history, the bank will want to examine your books and complete other due diligence.

Before applying, make sure all business records are complete and organized. If the bank approves your loan request, it will set up payment terms, including interest. If the process sounds a lot like the process you have gone through numerous times to receive a bank loan, you are right.

Advantages of Debt Financing

There are several advantages to financing your business through debt:

- The lending institution has no control over how you run your company, and it has no ownership.

- Once you pay back the loan, your relationship with the lender ends. That is especially important as your business becomes more valuable.

- The interest you pay on debt financing is tax deductible as a business expense.

- The monthly payment, as well as the breakdown of the payments, is a known expense that can be accurately included in your forecasting models.

Disadvantages of Debt Financing

However, debt financing for your business does come with some downsides:

- Adding a debt payment to your monthly expenses assumes that you will always have the capital inflow to meet all business expenses, including the debt payment. For small or early-stage companies that is often far from certain.

- Small business lending can be slowed during recessions. In tougher times for the economy, it can be difficult to receive debt financing unless you are overwhelmingly qualified.

During economic downturns, it can be much harder for small businesses to qualify for debt financing.

The U.S. Small Business Administration (SBA) works with certain banks to offer small business loans. A portion of the loan is guaranteed by the credit and full faith of the government of the United States. Designed to decrease the risk to lending institutions, these loans allow business owners who might not otherwise be qualified to receive debt financing. You can find more information about these and other SBA loans on the SBA's website.

What Is Equity Financing?

If you have ever watched ABC's hit series "Shark Tank," you may have a general idea of how equity financing works. It comes from investors, often called "venture capitalists" or "angel investors."

A venture capitalist is usually a firm rather than an individual. The firm has partners, teams of lawyers, accountants, and investment advisors who perform due diligence on any potential investment. Venture capital firms often deal in large investments ($3 million or more), and so the process is slow, and the deal is often complex.

Angel investors, by contrast, are normally wealthy individuals who want to invest a smaller amount of money into a specific product instead of building a business. They are perfect for somebody such as the software developer who needs a capital infusion to fund the development of their product. Angel investors move fast and want simple terms.

Equity financing uses an investor, not a lender; if you end up in bankruptcy, you do not owe anything to the investor, who, as a part owner of the business, simply loses their investment.

Advantages of Equity Financing

Funding your business through investors has several advantages:

- The biggest advantage is that you do not have to pay back the money. If your business enters bankruptcy, your investor or investors are not creditors. They are partial owners in your company, and, because of that, their money is lost along with your company.

- You do not have to make monthly payments, so there is often more liquid cash on hand for operating expenses.

- Investors understand that it takes time to build a business. You will get the money you need without the pressure of having to see your product or business thriving within a short amount of time.

Disadvantages of Equity Financing

Similarly, there are a number of disadvantages that come with equity financing:

- How do you feel about having a new partner? When you raise equity financing, it involves giving up ownership of a portion of your company. The larger and riskier the investment, the more of a stake the investor will want. You might have to give up 50% or more of your company. Unless you later construct a deal to buy the investor's stake, that partner will take 50% of your profits indefinitely.

- You will also have to consult with your investors before making decisions. Your company is no longer solely yours, and if an investor has more than 50% of your company, you have a boss to whom you must answer.

What Is Mezzanine Capital?

Put yourself in the position of the lender for a moment. The lender is looking for the best value for its money relative to the least amount of risk. The problem with debt financing is that the lender does not get to share in the success of the business. All it gets is its money back with interest while taking on the risk of default. That interest rate is not going to provide an impressive return by investment standards. It will offer single digit returns.

Mezzanine capital often combines the best features of equity and debt financing. Although there is no set structure for this type of business financing, debt capital often gives the lending institution the right to convert the loan to an equity interest in the company if you do not repay the loan on time or in full.

Advantages of Mezzanine Capital

Choosing to use mezzanine capital comes with several advantages:

- This type of loan is appropriate for a new company that is already showing growth. Banks are reluctant to lend to a company that does not have financial data. According to Dr. Ajay Tyagi's 2017 book Capital Investment and Financing for Beginners, Forbes has reported that bank lenders are often looking for at least three years of financial data. However, a newer business may not have that much data to supply. By adding an option to take an ownership stake in the company, the bank has more of a safety net, making it easier to get the loan.

- Mezzanine capital is treated as equity on the company's balance sheet. Showing equity rather than a debt obligation makes the company look more attractive to future lenders.

- Mezzanine capital is often provided very quickly with little due diligence.

Disadvantages of Mezzanine Capital

Mezzanine capital does have its share of disadvantages:

- The coupon or interest is often higher, as the lender views the company as elevated risk. Mezzanine capital provided to a business that already has debt or equity obligations is often subordinate to those obligations, increasing the risk that the lender will not be repaid. Because of the elevated risk, the lender may want to see a 20% to 30% return.

- Much like equity capital, the risk of losing a sizable portion of the company is very real.

Please note that mezzanine capital is not as standard as debt or equity financing. The deal, as well as the risk/reward profile, will be specific to each party.

Off-balance balance financing is good for one-time large purposes, allowing a business to create a special purpose vehicle (SPV) that carries the expense on its balance sheet, making the business seem less in debt.

Off-Balance Sheet Financing

Think about your personal finances for a minute. What if you were applying for a new home mortgage and discovered a way to create a legal entity that takes your student loan, credit card, and automobile debt off your credit report? Businesses can do that.

Off-balance sheet financing is not a loan. It is primarily a way to keep large purchases (debts) off a company's balance sheet, making it look stronger and less debt laden. For example, if the company needed an expensive piece of equipment, it could lease it instead of buying it or create a special purpose vehicle (SPV)—one of those "alternate families" that would hold the purchase on its balance sheet. The sponsoring company often overcapitalizes the SPV to make it look attractive should the SPV need a loan to service the debt.

Off-balance sheet financing is strictly regulated, and accepted accounting principles (GAAP) govern its use. This type of financing is not appropriate for most businesses, but it may become an option for small businesses that grow into much larger corporate structures.

Funding From Family and Friends

If your funding needs are small, you may want to first pursue fewer formal means of financing. Family and friends who believe in your business can offer simple and advantageous repayment terms in exchange for setting up a lending model like some of the more formal models. For example, you could offer them stock in your company or pay them back just as you would a debt financing deal, in which you make regular payments with interest.

Tapping Into Retirement Accounts

Whereas you may be able to borrow from your retirement plan and pay that loan back with interest, an alternative known as a Rollover for Business Startups (ROBS) has emerged as a practical source of funding for those who are starting a business. When executed properly, ROBS allow entrepreneurs to invest their retirement savings into a new business venture without incurring taxes, early withdrawal penalties, or loan costs. However, ROBS transaction are complex, so it is essential to work with an experienced and competent provider.

The Bottom Line

When you can avoid financing from a formal source, it will usually be more advantageous for your business. If you do not have family or friends with the means to help, debt financing is the easiest source of funds for small businesses. As your business grows or reaches later stages of product development, equity financing or mezzanine capital may become options. When it comes to financing and how it will affect your business, less is more.

Factor

What Is a Factor?

A factor is an intermediary agent that provides cash or financing to companies by purchasing their accounts receivables. A factor is a funding source that agrees to pay the company the value of an invoice less a discount for commission and fees. Factoring can help companies improve their short-term cash needs by selling their receivables in return for an injection of cash from the factoring company. The practice is also known as factoring, factoring finance, and accounts receivable financing.

Key Takeaways

- A factor is a funding source that agrees to pay a company the value of an invoice less a discount for commission and fees.

- The terms and conditions set by a factor may vary depending on its internal practices.

- The factor is more concerned with the creditworthiness of the invoiced party than the company from which it has purchased the receivable.

Watch Now: What Does Factor Mean in Financing?

How a Factor Works

Factoring allows a business to obtain immediate capital or money based on the future income attributed to a particular amount due on an account receivable or a business invoice. Accounts receivables represent money owed to the company from its customers for sales made on credit. For accounting purposes, receivables are recorded on the balance sheet as current assets since the money is usually collected in less than one year.

Sometimes companies can experience cash flow shortfalls when their short-term debts or bills exceed their revenue being generated from sales. If a company has a sizable portion of its sales done via accounts receivables, the money collected from the receivables might not be paid in time for the company to meet its short-term payables. As a result, companies can sell their receivables to a financial provider (called a factor) and receive cash.

There are three parties directly involved in a transaction involving a factor: the company selling its accounts receivables; the factor that purchases the receivables; and the company's customer, who must now pay the receivable amount to the factor instead of paying the company that was originally owed the money.

Requirements for a Factor

Although the terms and conditions set by a factor can vary depending on its internal practices, the funds are often released to the seller of the receivables within 24 hours. In return for paying the company cash for its accounts receivables, the factor earns a fee.

Typically, a percentage of the receivable amount is kept by the factor. However, that percentage can vary, depending on the creditworthiness of the customers paying the receivables. If the financial company acting as the factor believes there's increased risk of taking a loss due to the customers not being able to pay the receivable amounts, they will charge a higher fee to the company selling the receivables. If there is a minimal risk of taking a loss from collecting the receivables, the factor fee charged to the company will be lower.

The company selling the receivables is transferring the risk of default (or nonpayment) by its customers to the factor. As a result, the factor must charge a fee to help compensate for that risk. Also, how long the receivables have been outstanding or uncollected can impact the factor fee. The factoring agreement can vary between financial institutions. For example, a factor may want the company to pay additional money in the event one of the company's customers defaults on a receivable.

Benefits of a Factor

The company selling its receivables gets an immediate cash injection, which can help fund its business operations or improve its working capital. Working capital is vital to companies since it represents the difference between the short-term cash inflows (such as revenue) versus the short-term bills or financial obligations (such as debt payments). Selling, all or a portion, of its accounts receivables to a factor can help prevent a company, that's cash strapped, from defaulting on its loan payments with a creditor, such as a bank.

Although factoring is an expensive form of financing, it can help a company improve its cash flow. Factors provide a valuable service to companies that operate in industries where it takes a long time to convert receivables to cash—and to companies that are growing rapidly and need cash to take advantage of new business opportunities.

The factoring company also benefits since the factor can purchase uncollected receivables or assets at a discounted price in exchange for providing cash up front.

Factoring is not considered a loan, as the parties neither issue nor acquire debt as part of the transaction. The funds provided to the company in exchange for the accounts receivable are also not subject to any restrictions regarding use.

Example of a Factor

Assume a factor has agreed to purchase an invoice of $1 million from Clothing Manufacturers Inc., representing outstanding receivables from Behemoth Co. The factor negotiates to discount the invoice by 4% and will advance $720,000 to Clothing Manufacturers Inc. The balance of $240,000 will be forwarded by the factor to Clothing Manufacturers Inc. upon receipt of the $1 million accounts receivable invoice for Behemoth Co. The factor's fees and commissions from this factoring deal amount to $40,000. The factor is more concerned with the creditworthiness of the invoiced party, Behemoth Co., than the company from which it has purchased the receivables.

How Much Working Capital Does a Small Business Need?

It depends on business type, operating cycle, and management goals

The amount of working capital a small business needs to run smoothly depends on the type of business, its operating cycle, and the business owners' goals for future growth. However, while exceptionally large businesses can get by with negative working capital because of their ability to raise funds quickly, small businesses should maintain positive working capital figures.

Key Takeaways

- Working capital is the cash on hand used to keep a business operational, less liabilities and obligations.

- Depending on the line of business, working capital needs may be significant to procure raw materials and labor.

- Service businesses, on the other hand, rely far less on working capital and can operate with less overhead.

What Is Working Capital?

Working capital refers to the difference between a company's current assets and liabilities. Current assets are the things a business owns that can be turned into cash within the next 12 months, while current liabilities are the costs and expenses the business incurs within the same period. Common current assets include checking and savings accounts; marketable securities, such as stocks and bonds; inventory; and accounts receivable. Current liabilities include the cost of materials and supplies that need to be purchased to produce goods for sale, payments on short-term debt, rent, utilities, interest, and tax payments.

A company's working capital reflects its operational efficiency and budget management. If a business has more current liabilities than assets, its working capital is negative, meaning it may have difficulty meeting its financial obligations. A company with an extremely high working capital figure, conversely, is easily able to pay all its expenses with ample funding left over. Whether a given business requires high working capital is determined by three key factors: business type, operating cycle, and management goals.

Seasonal businesses require different amounts of working capital at various times of the year.

Business Type

Certain types of businesses require higher working capital than others. Businesses that have physical inventory, for example, often need considerable amounts of working capital to run smoothly.

This can include both retail and wholesale businesses, as well as manufacturers. Manufacturers must continuously purchase raw materials to produce inventory in house, while retailers and wholesalers must purchase premade inventory for sale to distributors or consumers.

In addition, many businesses are seasonal, meaning they require extremely high working capital during certain parts of the year as they ramp up for the busy season. Leading up to the winter holidays, for example, retail businesses such as department stores and grocery stores must increase inventory and staffing to accommodate the expected influx of customers.

Businesses that provide intangible products or services, such as consultants or online software providers, require much lower working capital. Businesses that have matured and are no longer looking to grow rapidly also have reduced need for working capital.

Operating Cycle

Ideally, a business can pay its short-term debts with revenue from sales. However, the length of a company's operating cycle can make this impossible. Companies that take a long time to create and sell a product need more working capital to ensure financial obligations incurred in the interim can be met. Similarly, companies that bill customers for goods or services already rendered rather than requiring payment up front need higher working capital in case collection on accounts receivable cannot be made in a timely manner.

Management Goals

The specific goals of the business owners are another crucial factor that determines the amount of working capital required by a small business. If the small business is new and looking to expand, a higher level of working capital is needed relative to that required by a small business intending to stay small. This is particularly true for businesses planning to expand product lines to venture into new markets, as the costs of research and development, design, and market research can be considerable.

How to Sell Stock in Your Company

You must know what you want and how to get it

- Details to Remember

- The Bottom Line

Starting and building a business is a rewarding endeavor for many entrepreneurs, but it is challenging work. All businesses require capital, and some require a significant amount. Sole ownership may not be the optimal structure when it comes to transitioning leadership, so many business owners sell ownership in their company through shares of stock.

Key Takeaways

- Selling stock shares in a sale of ownership can be done for multiple reasons, such as paying down debts, funding expansion, or helping to diversify an owner's risk.

- Depending on the business situation, owners can make a full or partial sale of ownership.

- Different options for selling a business include selling to private investors or to employees.

Reasons to Sell Stock in Your Company

There are many valid reasons to sell all or part of a business. Selling shares in a business can generate significant cash, which can pay down debts or be used for investments or charitable donations. That cash can also go back into the business, where it can fund expansion. Likewise, selling part of a business can reduce the owner's risk and allow them to diversify their personal assets.

Business owners may have several other reasons to sell shares. Selling shares over time can be a means of preparing for eventual succession and transferring ownership in a way that minimizes the tax shock to the eventual new owners. Finally, selling shares in a business can be the result of burnout or an unwillingness to grow the business further.

Complete vs. Partial Sale

First, you need to determine whether you are looking for a complete or partial sale. A complete sale is straightforward. It ends your involvement with the enterprise unless there is an employment or consulting contract that continues the relationship. Business sales can be structured in a way that offers annuity payments, so a complete sale makes sense if the owner is looking to completely move on financially.

Partial sales are different. They can raise capital, incentivize employees, or start ownership transitions. Before contemplating a partial sale, consider the ramifications of how much you wish to sell. If you sell too much and become a minority investor, you may no longer can control—or even influence—decisions.

Different Options for Selling

Going public

For most business owners, going public is not an option. Pursuing a public listing for your business is the most expensive option, and it is the most demanding in terms of legal, auditing, and disclosure requirements. Still, it is the best option for raising enormous amounts of capital and/or maximizing the value of a business.

Selling to large private investors

Companies do not have to go public to attract investment dollars from institutions. It is easier, faster, and cheaper to sell shares privately. While there are limits on the extent to which a company may solicit investors without filing with the Securities and Exchange Commission (SEC), private sales offer the same advantage of raising capital publicly without some of the downsides.1

Private sales usually include venture capital financing. In venture funding, a business or business owner sells shares to venture capital investors in exchange for capital that the business needs to grow or expand. In many cases significant share sales to large private investors also require that the company give the investors a spot on the board of directors.

Selling to smaller investors

In some respects, selling shares in your private business to small private investors is both more difficult and easier than selling to large, sophisticated investors. On the plus side, it is easier to handpick the investors, and there are often preexisting relationships. These investors are also less likely to force some of the more consequential compromises that bigger investors may demand, such as board representation or a chief executive officer (CEO) replacement. On the other hand, smaller investors typically have less money, and the legal process can be more complicated.

Selling to employees

Selling shares of your business to your employees is another option to consider. Establishing an employee stock ownership plan (ESOP) increases loyalty and retention and reduces a business' cash compensation needs—such as awards or bonuses—that would otherwise be paid in cash. These contributions are usually tax deductible. However, selling shares to employees is not a practical option for raising capital.

Selling shares of your business to your employees is a clever idea for a number of reasons, but raising capital is not one of them.

Important Steps in Selling a Business

If you are pondering an exit, here are some steps to get started.

Decide on your future

Begin by answering one question: How do you want to spend your time, money, and energy after you sell? Many people find this kind of soul-searching difficult and avoid it. Unfortunately, owners who enter negotiations with a potential buyer without a vision for the future rarely conclude the deal. Put your future life vision in a document, so you can refer to it when needed, and update it, as necessary.

Know what your shareholders want

The next question to ask is: What do your stakeholders want from your company? Stakeholders include people whose actions affect the health of the business—employees, other owners, investors, and family members. The goals of these pivotal people will shape the future of the business, and a smart buyer will want to know and agree with their objectives before concluding a deal.

Determine your business' value

Next, you need to establish a value for the business. This process may require the services of an accountant, an independent analyst, and/or a consultant. The entrepreneur has grown their business from an idea into an organization with employees, assets, intellectual property, and a reputation. It is priceless—to the entrepreneur. Potential buyers will assign a price to the business and walk away if they consider the owner's price outlandish.

If you are considering a sale to a third party, seek the assistance of a business broker, who will typically be experienced in finding a buyer, managing paperwork, navigating tax and other laws, and closing the deal more quickly than an entrepreneur selling a business for the first time. A broker will concentrate on the sale, allowing the entrepreneur to continue to focus on running—and maintaining the value of—their business.

Once you have an idea of the fair value of the business, solicit multiple bids (at least three if possible). If the bids differ significantly from the owner's idea of fair value, it may well be necessary to rethink the assumptions.

It is also worth mentioning that private businesses always sell at discounts to public companies, but a controlling stake is often worth a substantial premium to noncontrolling minority investors.

Create a marketing strategy

It is also important to properly market a business that is to be sold. There are internet sites that traffic in helping owners to sell their businesses, but owners need to be prepared to create their own sales materials. At a minimum, a well-formatted, one-page summary is critical, as is a more detailed package for serious bidders. These materials need to include items such as the sales, profits, and cash flows of the business, as well as a comprehensive description of the business and its assets.

Get your business in order

Finally, get the business in order before attempting to sell it. Just as a house needs a refresh before a sale, so does a business. Look for issues that will scare off potential buyers and fix them before opening the books for inspection. Make sure that cosmetic details and repairs are attended to, prepare a thorough inventory and equipment list, and have multiple years of financial data and tax returns on hand.

Remember that selling your business is a process that will take time, not a singular event.

Other Details to Remember

There are several other key details to keep in mind when considering selling part or all your business. Remember that it takes time. An initial public offering (IPO) or venture round of financing takes months to organize and getting a competitive price for a personal business can take a year or more. Patience is vital; the more you rush to sell, the worse the prices you will see.

Chris Snider, CEO and president of Exit Planning Institute, a national organization that trains financial advisors on the fundamentals of selling a business, says that selling should be treated like retirement and started early. "Exit planning is a process, not an event," Snider says. "It's a way of running your business that maximizes its value and provides a means of achieving an owner's personal and financial goals." As good as Snider's advice sounds, many entrepreneurs fail to follow it. Instead, they treat selling their business like an event approached when they are ready to retire, burned out, or facing an unexpected life change.

It is also important to contemplate and plan for the tax and cash flow consequences of a sale. Investors are likely to insist on more-rigorous auditing or reporting. What is more, if you sell shares with the promise of regular dividends, you need to prove the cash flow to support them. Consult with accountants and/or lawyers regarding the potential tax consequences of a sale—both to you and the business.

Finally, do not forget to consider the psychological implications. Are you ready to walk away? Are you prepared to have new partners questioning your decisions? Having investors in your business makes you legally accountable to others and requires more transparency than a sole proprietor may be accustomed to.

The Bottom Line

Selling even a small part of your business is a serious undertaking. At a minimum, make sure you are thoroughly prepared and have clear expectations for the process. Selling shares in a confidential business can be a wonderful way to raise capital, incentivize employees, or bring new talent and ideas into a business, but it requires patience, preparedness, and a willingness to negotiate.

The best way to get the maximum value from selling your company is to plan well in advance. Take a hard look at what your business is worth and solve any problems that could make it sell for less than it should. Then take the proceeds and start on your next adventure.

How SBA Loans Can Help Your Small Business

Turn to the SBA for everything from COVID-19 relief to expansion funds

Information in this article reflects congressional funding as well as guidance from the Small Business Administration following passage of the Consolidated Appropriations Act (CAA), 2021, on Dec. 27, 2020, and the American Rescue Plan Act of 2021, signed into law on March 11, 2021.

Whether you are seeking financial help for your small business in response to the coronavirus (COVID-19) pandemic or simply wondering how to obtain financing to expand, a loan from the Small Business Administration (SBA) may be just the solution that you need.

Low-interest, long-term SBA loans are a viable option for business owners suffering substantial disaster-related physical or economic damage or who want to grow their business and cannot obtain other nongovernment financing.

Key Takeaways

- Legislation enacted on Dec. 27, 2020, provides new funding for the Paycheck Protection Program (PPP) and Economic Injury Disaster Loan (EIDL) programs, along with funding for forgivable EIDL Targeted Advances and Shuttered Venue Operator (SVO) Grants.

- The American Rescue Plan, signed into law on March 11, 2021, provides additional small business funding and guidance.

- The PPP Extension Act, signed by President Biden on March 30, 2021, extends the application deadline for PPP loans to May 31, 2021, continues the covered period for PPP loans through June 30, 2021, and allows lenders to process PPP loans through June 30, 2021, as well.

- PPP loans are provided by private lenders, while EIDL loans and SVO Grants are generated with funds provided by the government.

- SBA business expansion loans are guaranteed loans with funds coming from approved private lenders.

- Additional SBA programs include Express Bridge Loans, 7(a) Debt Relief Loans, Loan Deferrals, and several others.

Consolidated Appropriations Act, 2021 & American Rescue Plan Act of 2021

Neither the Consolidated Appropriations Act (CAA), 2021 nor the American Rescue Plan Act of 2021 are government loan programs per se. They are laws, passed by Congress, which provide additional funding and rule changes for several government programs, including the Paycheck Protection Program (PPP), Economic Injury Disaster Loan (EIDL) program, and EIDL advances. Also included is funding for a new Shuttered Venue Operator (SVO) Grant program.

Descriptions of the programs below reflect changes made by the CAA and the American Rescue Plan. Additional guidance from the Treasury Department and the SBA may require further updates.12

Paycheck Protection Program (PPP)

The Paycheck Protection Program (PPP), created by the Coronavirus Aid, Relief, and Economic

Security (CARES) Act on March 27, 2020, provides forgivable SBA emergency 7(a) loans of up to $10 million to small businesses with 500 or fewer employees, including sole proprietorships, independent contractors, and self-employed people affected by COVID-19.

This program was amended by the PPP Flexibility Act of 2020, with new guidelines that allow full or partial forgiveness if at least **60%** (formerly 75%) of the amount forgiven was used for payroll and **40%** (formerly 25%) of the amount forgiven was used for mortgage interest, rent, and utilities.

Instead of a six-month payment deferral, your loan is deferred until the SBA remits the forgiven amount to your lender. If you do not seek forgiveness, then your payments are deferred for 10 months from the end of the covered period.

As with the original PPP program, no collateral is required, and the loan does not carry any fees. However, instead of a two-year term, you now have five years to pay off your loan at the same 1% fixed rate as before.

The PPP Flexibility Act of 2020 further stipulates that if you make a good faith offer to rehire a furloughed employee (same hours, same wages) and documented it, then you can exclude that employee from your count for purposes of forgiveness if they refuse your offer.

The PPP loan program, which stopped accepting loan applications on Aug. 8, 2020, due to lack of funds, received new funding via the Consolidated Appropriations Act, 2021, and the American Rescue Plan Act of 2021.

Paycheck Protection Program (PPP) Loan Refresh

The Consolidated Appropriations Act and the American Rescue Plan provide additional funding and guidance for the PPP loan program. Presidential executive orders have also helped target funds where they are needed most.

Changes to the PPP Made by the Consolidated Appropriations Act, 2021

The Consolidated Appropriations Act, 2021 provides $284 billion in new PPP loan funding through March 31, 2021, including special set-asides for companies in depressed areas and those with 10 or fewer employees.

The legislation provides first-time forgivable PPP loans of up to $10 million for qualifying companies with 500 employees or fewer and second-draw loans of up to $2 million for previous borrowers with 300 or fewer employees.

If you return all or part of your PPP loan, then you may reapply for the maximum amount applicable—provided you have not already received forgiveness. Further, if you would be eligible for a higher loan amount due to interim final rule changes, then you can work with your lender to modify the amount of your loan—even after forgiveness.

The list of forgivable expenses has been expanded and now includes:

- Personal protective equipment (PPE).

- Complying with federal or state health and safety guidelines.

- Software, cloud computing, and other human resources and accounting needs; and

- Property damage due to public disturbances that took place in 2020 and were not covered by insurance.

Also new, expenses that you pay with PPP loan proceeds are now tax-deductible even if the loan is forgiven. This applies to both first- and second-draw loans.

You can now select a covered period between eight and 24 weeks from when you receive your loan, instead of needing to pick either eight or 24 weeks. Your covered period can extend through March 31, 2021.

New, simplified applications for loans under $150,000 and for forgiveness of those loans are now available.

You no longer must deduct your $10,000 Economic Injury Disaster Loan (EIDL) advance from the forgivable amount of your PPP loan, and the new legislation directs the SBA to treat previous PPP loans and EIDL advances the same.

Changes to the PPP Loan Program That Target Very Small Businesses

On Feb. 22, 2021, the Biden administration announced several changes to the PPP program designed to make PPP funds available to the smallest businesses, including some excluded from previous relief efforts.

- Beginning Feb. 24, 2021, businesses with fewer than 20 employees will have an exclusive two-week window to apply for PPP funding. During this period, larger businesses will not be allowed to apply.

- The formula used to calculate PPP loans has been revised to allow sole proprietors, independent contractors, and self-employed individuals to receive more financial support.

- Eligibility rules have been changed to let small business owners with non-fraud-related felonies receive PPP loans if the applicant is not incarcerated at the time of the application.

- Also, newly eligible are those who are delinquent on federal student loans.

- Non-citizen small business owners who are lawful U.S. residents, including Green Card holders and those here on a visa, also will be eligible and allowed to use their Individual Taxpayer Identification Numbers (ITINs) to apply for PPP relief.

Changes to PPP Made by the American Rescue Plan Act of 2021

When the American Rescue Plan Act was signed into law on March 11, 2021, it provided $7.25 billion for PPP forgivable loans.1 Additional legislation known as the PPP Extension Act of 2021, signed by President Biden on March 30, 2021, lets business owners apply for a PPP loan through May 31, 2021, extends the covered period for PPP through June 30, 2021, and allows lenders to process PPP loans through that date.

The American Rescue Plan Act further enhances the PPP program by:

- Making more not-for-profits eligible for the PPP by creating a new category called "additional covered nonprofit entity."

- Widening PPP eligibility to include 501(c)(3) organizations and veterans' organizations that employ not more than 500 employees per physical location.

- Including 501(c)(6) organizations, domestic marketing organizations, and additional covered not-for-profit entities that employ not more than 300 employees per physical location.

- Allocating $15 billion for targeted Economic Injury Disaster Loan (EIDL) advance payments. Provides funds to businesses located in low-income communities that have no more than 300 employees and have suffered an economic loss of more than 30%, as determined by the amount that the entity's gross receipts declined during an eight-week period, between March 2, 2020, and Dec. 31, 2021, relative to a comparable eight-week period immediately preceding March 2, 2020.

- Ruling that funds from Targeted EIDL Advances shall not be included in the gross income of the person who receives the grant and that no tax deductions will be denied, no tax attribute reduced, and no basis increase denied due to the exclusion of the grant funds from gross income.

- Instituting the Restaurant Revitalization Fund: $28.6 billion for restaurants, bars, and other eligible providers of food and drink. It allows for grants equal to the pandemic-related revenue loss of the eligible entity, up to $10 million per entity, or $5 million per physical location. The grants are calculated by subtracting 2020 revenue from 2019 revenue. Entities are limited to 20 locations.

- $1.25 billion for shuttered venue operators.

- $175 million to create a "community navigator" pilot program to increase awareness of and participation in COVID-19 relief programs for business owners currently lacking access, with priority for businesses owned by socially and economically disadvantaged individuals, women, and veterans.

Where to Apply for an SBA Paycheck Protection Program (PPP) Loan

Apply for this loan through any existing SBA 7(a) lender or through any participating federally insured depository institution, federally insured credit union, and Farm Credit System institution. Start by consulting with your local lender to see if it is participating.

The SBA and the Treasury Department announced that the PPP would reopen the week of Jan. 11, 2021, for new borrowers and existing PPP loan recipients.

Initially, only community financial institutions, including community development financial institutions (CDFIs), minority depository institutions (MDIs), certified development companies, and microloan intermediaries were able to make first-draw PPP loans beginning Jan. 11, 2021. Second-draw PPP loans through the same lenders started Jan. 13, 2021. First- and second-draw loans were available from small lenders with less than $1 billion in assets as of Jan. 15, 2021, and all participating PPP lenders were approved to make loans beginning Jan. 19, 2021.

Do not use any other road to apply for a PPP loan; scammers will offer shortcuts to PPP loans, just as they did with the original program. The Federal Trade Commission filed a case against one such company on April 17, 2020. Only apply by first going to the SBA website. And know that the SBA will never ask for Social Security numbers—or bank account or credit card numbers—up front, the FTC cautioned.

Economic Injury Disaster Loan (EIDL) Advance

Small business owners in all 50 states, Washington, D.C., and U.S. territories were able to apply for an Economic Injury Disaster Loan (EIDL) Advance of up to $10,000 as part of the application process for an EIDL loan. The loan advance did not have to be repaid, and you did not actually have to be approved for an EIDL loan to receive the advance; however, the amount of the loan advance was deducted from total loan eligibility.

The EIDL Advance program ended July 11, 2020, due to lack of funds. A new EIDL Targeted Advance program was created with passage of the Consolidated Appropriations Act (CAA), 2021.

Economic Injury Disaster Loan (EIDL) Targeted Advance Refresh

The Targeted EIDL Advance program, which is more restrictive than its predecessor, is authorized under the CAA and makes up to $10,000 available to applicants located in low-income communities who previously received an EIDL Advance for less than $10,000, or those who applied but received no funds due to lack of program funding.

If you previously **received** a partial EIDL Advance ($1,000 to $9,000), then the SBA will reach out to you first by official (@sba.gov) email to determine your eligibility and provide instructions.

If you are in this group, then you may qualify if you:

- Are in a low-income community, as defined in section 45D(e) of the Internal Revenue Code; and

- Can demonstrate that you suffered a more than 30% reduction in revenue during an eight-week period beginning on March 2, 2020, or later. You will be asked to provide proof of the more than 30% revenue reduction.

If you previously **applied for** an EIDL Advance but did not receive one due to a lack of funds, then you are next in line to be contacted by the SBA.

To qualify in this group, you must meet the qualifications above plus:

- Have no more than 300 employees.

If your business is otherwise eligible for the EIDL program—including if you are a sole proprietor, independent contractor, or private, nonprofit organization—and you meet the qualifications above, then you are eligible for consideration for the targeted advance. Agricultural enterprises are not eligible.

You may be asked to provide an Internal Revenue Service (IRS) Form 4506-T giving the SBA permission to request your tax return information.

Do not submit a duplicate COVID-19 EIDL application. Only prior applicants will be considered for the Targeted EIDL Advance.

Economic Injury Disaster Loan (EIDL)

SBA Coronavirus Disaster assistance loans are designed to help businesses recover from the economic effects of COVID-19. Disaster assistance loans of up to $500,000 with maximum terms of 30 years are available. Small business owners in all 50 states, Washington, D.C., and U.S. territories are eligible to apply.

Loans can be used to pay fixed debts, payroll, accounts payable, and other bills that cannot be paid due to the impact of COVID-19. The interest rate for small businesses is 3.75%. Nonprofits pay just 2.75%.

On March 24, 2021, the SBA announced that starting April 6, 2021, it would raise the EIDL limit from $150,000 covering six months of economic injury to $500,000 for 24 months of economic injury.

Economic Injury Disaster Loan (EIDL) Refresh

The main change brought about by the CAA, aside from $20 billion in additional funding for the Economic Injury Disaster Loan (EIDL) program, was an extension of time to file for a loan from Dec. 31, 2020, to Dec. 31, 2021.

On March 24, 2021, the SBA raised the EIDL limit from $150,000 covering six months of economic injury to $500,000 for 24 months of economic injury, effective April 6, 2021. Further, some businesses that previously received a loan under the lower limits may be deemed eligible to increase their loan amount. The SBA said it would notify those businesses of their eligibility.

The SBA anticipates opening applications for Shuttered Venue Operator (SVO) Grants beginning April 8, 2021.

Shuttered Venue Operator (SVO) Grant program

The Shuttered Venue Operators (SVO) Grant program, authorized by the CAA on Dec. 27, 2020, includes $15 billion in grants to shuttered venues. Funds are administered by the SBA's Office of

Disaster Assistance.

Eligible applicants can qualify for SVO Grants equal to 45% of their gross earned revenue, with a maximum of $10 million. There is $2 billion reserved for eligible applicants with up to 50 full-time employees.

Eligible entities include:

- Live venue operators or promoters

- Theatrical producers

- Live performing arts organization operators

- Relevant museum operators, zoos, and aquariums that meet specific criteria

- Motion picture theater operators

- Talent representatives, and

- Any business entity owned by an eligible entity that also meets eligibility requirements

SVO Grants are only available to venues that:

- Have been in operation as of Feb. 29, 2020

- Have not received a PPP loan on or after Dec. 27, 2020

SVO Grand funds may be used for: payroll, rent, utility, mortgage payments, debt, worker protection, payments to independent contractors, maintenance, administrative costs, state and local taxes, operating leases (in effect as of Feb. 15, 2020), insurance, advertising, and other costs of production.

Grantees may not use funds to purchase real estate, make loan payments on loans originated after Feb. 15, 2020, make investments, or make political contributions or payments.

Where to Apply for Coronavirus Disaster Assistance

Economic Injury Disaster Assistance Loans and Targeted Advances are funded by the Small Business Administration (SBA). Your application for an EIDL loan goes through the SBA website.

Recall that there is no application process for the new EIDL $10,000 Targeted Advance. The SBA will contact you if you are eligible.

The SBA expects to open SVO Grant applications on April 8, 2021. Interested entities can stay up to date by visiting www.sba.gov/svogrant on a regular basis.

SBA Express Bridge Loan (EBL)

If you already have a business relationship with an SBA Express Lender, then a new Express

Bridge Loan Pilot Program offers a quick turnaround on up to $25,000 to help bridge the gap until your SBA Economic Injury Disaster Loan (EIDL) is approved. Bridge funds can be paid in full or in part with proceeds from your EIDL once it is approved.

Where to apply for an SBA Express Bridge Loan

Consult the Express Bridge Loan Pilot Program Guide or contact your local SBA district office for details.

SBA 7(a) Loan Debt Relief

The SBA Debt Relief program will pay principal, interest, and fees for six months on new 7(a), 504, and microloans made from March 27, 2020, to Sept. 27, 2020. The program also will pay principal, interest, and fees for six months on existing 7(a), 504, and microloans beginning with the first payment due after March 27, 2020.

Where to apply for 7(a) Loan Debt Relief

This relief is automatic and does not require an application. Check with your lender for more information or if you have questions.

SBA Deferral on Existing Home and Business Loans

If you currently have an SBA Serviced Disaster (Home and Business) Loan that was in "regular servicing" on March 1, 2020, then the SBA is providing automatic deferral on your loan through March 31, 2021. Note the following:

- Interest will continue to accrue on your loan during the deferral period.

- 1201 monthly notices will still be mailed but will show no payment due.

- Pre-Authorized Debit (PAD) payments will not automatically be canceled. You must contact your servicer to do that.

- You may continue making payments if you wish. No contact is necessary.

- After the deferral period, you must resume payments and set up PAD if you canceled it earlier.

Where to apply for existing disaster loan deferral

Deferral is automatic. You do not need to apply. After the deferral period, you do not need to contact the SBA before resuming payments.

SBA Business Expansion Loans

The disaster-related loans referenced above are made with funds appropriated or guaranteed by Congress. SBA business expansion loans are commercial loans, structured according to SBA requirements, with an SBA guarantee. Small business owners and borrowers who have access to other financing with reasonable terms are not eligible for this type of SBA-guaranteed loan. Guaranteed loan programs from the SBA include the following:

7(a) Loan Program

This is the SBA's most common loan program and provides financial help for businesses with specific requirements, such as franchises, farms and agricultural businesses, and fishing vessels. There is no minimum loan amount, but the maximum is $5 million. Note that emergency SBA 7(a) loans available under the PPP have different requirements from those used for business expansion.

There are nine types of 7(a) loans—each with its own maximum loan amount, SBA guarantee, negotiated interest rate, and other factors—all of which are spelled out on the 7(a)-loan program web page.

Microloan Program

This program provides small, short-term loans of up to $50,000 to small businesses and certain types of not-for-profit childcare centers. Loans can be used to buy new equipment, supplies, or furniture, or to provide working capital. Loans are provided by microlenders, with each having its own lending and credit requirements.

CDC/504 Program

This loan program provides financing for businesses to purchase real estate, major fixed assets, and equipment, or to make improvements like landscaping. This program can also provide funding for renovation.

Where to apply for an expansion loan

As previously noted, the SBA does not lend money directly to help you grow your business, as it does when provide disaster relief. Instead, it sets stipulations for loans made by its partners (lenders, community development organizations, and microlending institutions). You can apply for an expansion loan at any SBA-approved lender or use the SBA's Lender Match.

4 Steps to Getting a Small Business Loan Without Collateral

The financing is available, but loan terms and approval requirements vary widely

When you need a small-business loan—either to fund your next stage of growth or to keep your business on solid ground during an unexpected crisis—one thing to consider is whether you'll be expected to bring collateral to the table. Collateral acts as security for the lender if you default on the loan and cannot repay it for any reason. If your business is short on assets that could be pledged as security, finding a no-collateral business loan may be your top priority.

Fortunately, it's possible to find business loans that don't require collateral as a condition for approval. Before applying for one of these loans, it is important to do your research, so you know what to expect.

Key Takeaways

- It is possible to find unsecured business loans through the Small Business Administration and online lenders.

- No collateral does not mean that you will not be required to assume some level of personal fiscal responsibility for business debt.

- Peer-to-peer lending is another option for pursuing business loans with no collateral requirements.

- Lenders may charge higher fees or interest rates for no-collateral business loans.

1. Know Your Options for No-Collateral Business Loans

The first step in getting a business loan requiring no collateral is to know which options are available. No-collateral loans are offered by a variety of lenders, but loan terms and approval requirements can be quite different.

SBA 7(a) Loans

The Small Business Administration (SBA) guarantees loans for small-business owners through its network of partner lenders. There are several SBA loan programs you might consider when you need working capital, with the 7(a) program being one of the most popular. The SBA 7(a) program does not require collateral for loans of up to $25,000, which is helpful if you only need to borrow a smaller amount of money.

For loans greater than $350,000, the SBA requires lenders to collateralize loans to the maximum extent possible, up to the loan amount. If you do not have sufficient business assets to fully secure the loan, lenders can use personal real estate you own as collateral. Still, not having any collateral at all is not a barrier to getting a 7(a) loan if you meet the other requirements.

SBA Disaster Loans

In addition to 7(a) loans, the SBA offers disaster relief loans for businesses that experience losses associated with natural disasters as well as economic crises. So, for example, a business that's experienced losses due to a government mandate to shut down could apply for an economic injury loan.

Like 7(a) loans, disaster loans under $25,000 do not require collateral. If you are borrowing more than that amount, collateral is expected, but, again, the SBA will not deny you for a loan based on lack of collateral alone.

If you are applying for an SBA loan to purchase equipment, you may be expected to offer up to 10% of the purchase price in cash as a down payment.

Online and Alternative Small Business Loans

Online and alternative lenders can offer a variety of loans without collateral requirements to help you meet your business' working-capital needs. The types of financing you may be able to get without having to provide collateral up front include:

- Term Loan

- Invoice Financing (also known as "accounts receivable financing")

- Inventory Financing

- Merchant Cash Advance

- Equipment Financing

- Purchase Order Financing

- Line of Credit

With these types of small-business financing, there may be some type of security required, but it is not cash or another physical asset you have to offer. For example, with invoice financing, you are leveraging your outstanding invoices to borrow money. With a merchant cash advance, you are borrowing against the value of your future credit card receipts. And in the case of equipment financing, the equipment you are buying, or leasing serves as collateral for the loan.

Peer-to-peer lending is another option for small-business financing that does not require collateral. Peer-to-peer lending platforms connect investors with small-business owners who need loans. Investors pool money together to fund the loan, and owners pay it back the same as any other loan, with interest. These loans are unsecured, meaning there is no collateral needed.

2. Review Your Business Financials to Determine Whether You Qualify

Some types of no-collateral small-business financing may be more difficult to qualify for than others. With an SBA 7(a) loan, for instance, you must have at least two years of operating history under your belt, meet the SBA's definition of an eligible small business, and have the minimum credit score and revenues SBA lenders look for. The SBA also requires that you exhaust all other borrowing options first before applying for a 7(a) loan.

With online and alternative lenders, on the other hand, the requirements may be more fluid. For example, a lower credit score may not be an obstacle to getting a merchant cash advance or invoice financing. And it may be easier to get startup loans from online or alternative lenders that only require six months of operating history.

The second step in getting a business loan with no collateral requirements is evaluating your business and its overall financial position. That means doing things like:

- Checking your personal and business credit scores

- Updating your balance sheet

- Creating key financial documents, such as a profit and loss statement and a cash flow statement

- Reviewing your business expenses and overall cash flow

The purpose is twofold: to determine your creditworthiness for a loan and to assess your ability to pay it back. Failing to repay a loan can damage your credit score, making it more difficult to obtain any type of financing in the future.

Some types of no-collateral loans—such as a merchant cash advance or invoice financing—use a factor rate rather than an interest rate to determine the cost of borrowing. Depending on the financing terms and how quickly it is repaid, the factor rate can easily translate to a two- or three-digit effective APR.

3. Be Prepared for a Personal Guarantee or UCC Lien Instead

While you may be able to get a small business loan without having to offer collateral, that doesn't mean the lender won't ask for other conditions. Specifically, you may be asked to sign a personal guarantee or agree to a Uniform Commercial Code (UCC) lien.

A personal guarantee is what it sounds like: an agreement that you will personally repay the debt taken on by your business. Personal guarantees are often a requirement for no-collateral loans and small-business credit cards. As the lender has no collateral it can attach if you do not pay, the guarantee gives it leeway to sue you personally to collect an unpaid debt.4

A Uniform Commercial Code lien is a little different. This is a blanket lien that allows a lender to attach any or all your business assets if you default on a loan. So even though you did not put any collateral on the table to get the loan, a UCC lien will give the lender a backdoor option for attaching assets if you fail to pay.

4. Consider the Terms Carefully Before Signing

If you have applied for a small-business loan without collateral and have been approved, the last step is understanding the loan terms and conditions. When reviewing the loan agreement, pay attention to the interest rate and annual percentage rate (APR), the payment schedule, and the loan term. You need to know how long it will take you to pay the loan off and what your total cost of borrowing adds up to when the interest and fees are factored in.

Speaking of fees, check to see which fees you are being charged. For instance, which might include a loan origination fee or prepayment penalty. If your cash flow allows you to pay off the loan early, you do not want to pay a penalty to do it.

Finally, consider whether a personal guarantee or UCC lien is required as part of your borrowing agreement. While you may have the best of intentions to repay the loan, it is important to understand how these requirements might affect your business if you are unable to hold up your end of the bargain for any reason.

5 Biggest Challenges Facing Your Small Business

To overcome them you must know what they are

Starting a business is a significant achievement for many entrepreneurs, but maintaining one is the larger challenge. There are many familiar challenges every business face, whether they are large or small. These include hiring the right people, building a brand, developing a customer base, and so on. However, some are strictly small business problems, ones most large companies grew out of long ago.

Here are the five most significant challenges for small businesses.

Key Takeaways

- A small business should not allow itself to become dependent on a single client.

- Having professional help with money management frees up a small business owner to focus on operating concerns.

- It is essential to find the right balance between working long hours and business success.

- A small business owner should not create a situation where the business could not continue in their absence.

- Starting a small business may be different than simply working as a freelancer.

5 Biggest Challenges Facing Your Small Business

1. Client Dependence

If a single client makes up more than half of your income, you are more independent contractor than a business owner. Diversifying your client base is vital to growing a business, but it can be difficult, especially when the client in question pays well and is on time. Having a client willing to pay on time for a product or service is a godsend for many small businesses.

Unfortunately, this can result in a longer-term handicap because, even if you have employees and so on, you may still be acting as a subcontractor for a more significant business. This arrangement allows the client to avoid the risks of adding payroll in an area where the work may dry up at any time, and all that risk is transferred from the larger company to you and your employees. This arrangement can work if your main client has a consistent need for your product or service.

2. Money Management

Having enough cash to cover the bills is necessary for any business, but it is also necessary for every individual. Whether your business or your life, one will emerge as a capital drain that puts pressure on the other. To avoid this problem, small business owners must either be heavily capitalized or pick up extra income to shore up cash reserves when needed. Therefore, many small businesses start with the founders working a job and building a business simultaneously. While this split focus can make it challenging to grow a business, running out of cash makes growing a business impossible.

Money management becomes even more important when cash is flowing into the business. Although handling business accounting and taxes may be within the capabilities of most business owners, professional help is usually a promising idea. The complexity of a company's books increases with each client and employee, so getting an assist on the bookkeeping can prevent it from becoming a reason not to expand.

3. Fatigue

The hours, the work, and the constant pressure to perform wear on even the most passionate individuals. Many business owners—even successful ones—get stuck working much longer hours than their employees. Moreover, they fear their business will stall in their absence, so they avoid taking any time away from work to recharge.

Fatigue can lead to rash decisions about the business, including the desire to abandon it altogether. Finding a pace that keeps the business humming without grinding down the owner is a challenge that comes early (and often) in the evolution of a small business.

It is better for a business to have a diversified client base to pick up the slack when any single client quits paying.

4. Founder Dependence

If you get hit by a car, is your business still producing income the next day? A business that cannot operate without its founder is a business with a deadline. Many businesses suffer from founder dependence, and it is often caused by the founder being unable to let go of certain decisions and responsibilities as the business grows.

In theory, meeting this challenge is easy—a business owner merely must give over more control to employees or partners. In practice, however, this is a significant obstacle for founders because it usually involves compromising (at least initially) on the quality of work being done until the person doing the work learns the ropes.

Growth should never be the enemy of quality. A small business need both.

5. Balancing Quality and Growth

Even when a business is not founder-dependent, there comes a time when the issues from growth seem to match or even outweigh the benefits. Whether a service or a product, at some point, a business must sacrifice to scale up. This may mean not being able to personally manage every client relationship or not inspecting every widget.

Unfortunately, it is usually that level of personal engagement and attention to detail that makes a business successful. Therefore, many small business owners find themselves tied to these habits to the detriment of their development. There is a large middle ground between shoddy work and an unhealthy obsession with quality; it is up to the business owner to navigate its processes toward a compromise that allows growth without hurting the brand.

The Bottom Line

The problems faced by small businesses are considerable, and one of the worst things a would-be owner can do is go into business without considering the challenges ahead. We have looked at ways to help make these challenges more accessible, but there is no avoiding them.

On the other hand, a competitive drive is often one of the reasons people start their own business, and every challenge represents another opportunity to compete.

5 Ways to Keep Your Business Going in Hard Times

These general tips apply to all and can help a lot

Keeping a small business afloat in tough economic times is challenging. Unfortunately, there is no set playbook to follow to ride out the storm and right the ship. Every small business is different, and each carries its own risks and rewards. These differences make copying another company's turnaround strategy to the letter unrealistic. Still, there are some general strategies business owners can follow to help them stop taking on water and start bailing themselves out.

Key Takeaways

- Keeping a small business afloat in challenging times can be difficult, but extra attention to detail can help ensure that a business survives.

- Because every small business is different, and each carries its own risks and rewards, there is no set playbook to follow for survival.

- Some useful advice that applies across small businesses includes looking at the big picture, inventorying the staff, making sure the business has ready access to cash, sweating the small stuff, and avoiding a sacrifice of quality.

1. Look at the Big Picture

People tend to attack the most obvious immediate problems with vigor and without hesitation. That is understandable and might make good business sense in some situations. However, it is also advisable to step back and look at the big picture to see what is still working and what might need changing. It's an opportunity to better comprehend the size and scope of existing problems and further understand your company's business model—determining how its strengths and weaknesses come into play.

For example, suppose a small business owner discovers that two employees are consistently making mistakes with inventory that cause certain supplies to be overstocked or understocked. While an initial reaction might be to fire those employees, it could be wiser to examine whether the manager who hired and supervises them has professionally trained them.

If the manager is to blame, that person could be fired, but this might not be the best approach. If the manager's relationships with existing clientele have a history of bringing in repeat business and substantial revenue, they are someone you would want to keep. Retraining might be a better alternative than termination.

By thoroughly scrutinizing the strengths and weaknesses of the employees, the owner is looking at the issue from a top-down perspective, reducing or eliminating the chance that the problems will recur while avoiding a change that could adversely impact future sales.

Fix a similar kind of lens on analyzing how your product or service fits into the marketplace now, how the economic crisis has affected your customers and suppliers, and all the other key aspects of your business. You need to know how well your business model fits the current environment and forecast what various alternative scenarios of the future might mean for it.

2. Inventory Your Staff

Payroll is often one of the top costs a small business owner has, so seeing to it that the money is well spent makes sense. This may involve a thorough review of the staff—both when a problem arises and during the normal course of business—to make sure the right people are on board and doing their jobs effectively.

Both small business owners and large corporations tend to be penny wise and pound foolish when they hire the least expensive workers. Sometimes the productivity of those workers may be suspect. Hiring one worker who costs 20% more than the average worker but works 40% more effectively makes sense, particularly during periods of crisis. By constantly seeking résumés and interviews from new people, business owners can make changes to staff when needed to increase efficiency.

Low salaries can be counterproductive if they result in indifferent productivity.

3. Ensure Access to Cash

Small business owners should take steps to ensure that the company has access to cash, particularly in periods of crisis. Visiting a bank loan officer and understanding what's required to obtain a loan is a good first step, as is opening a line of credit in advance to fund possible short-term cash-flow problems. Establishing a good relationship with a banker is always useful for a small business.

Small business owners should have other potential sources of capital lined up as well. This might include tapping into savings, liquidating stock holdings, or borrowing from family members. A small business owner must have access to capital or have a creative way to obtain funds to make it through lean times.

4. Start Sweating the Small Stuff

Although it is important to keep an eye on the big picture, a small business owner should not overlook smaller things that may have an adverse impact on the business. A large tree obstructing the public's view of the business or the company's signage, inadequate parking, lack of road/traffic access, and ineffective advertising are examples of small problems that can put a big dent in a business' bottom line.

Considering and analyzing the numerous factors that bring customers in the door can help to identify some problems. Going through your quarterly expenses line by line may also help. Owners should not be checking for one-time expenses here, as those items were necessary charges. Instead, they should look for small items that seem innocent but are draining the accounts.

For example, the cost of office supplies can quickly get out of hand if they are ordered improperly. Similarly, if your supplier increases product prices, you should consider looking around for a cheaper supplier.

5. Do not Sacrifice Quality

Keeping a handle on costs is crucial in tough times. Owners need to stay on the offensive and get employees on board with changes that are being made. However, be cognizant of not sacrificing quality when making these product changes.

Business owners seeking to improve profit margins should be wary of making dramatic changes to key components. For example, if a pizzeria is going through a dry spell, the owner could seek to expand margins per pie by purchasing cheaper cheese or sauce ingredients. Note that the strategy could backfire if customers become dissatisfied with the taste of the pizza and sales decrease. The key is to make cost and other cuts that do not compromise the quality of the finished product. There is a way to cut the price of takeout boxes or paper napkins instead.

7 Popular Marketing Techniques for Small Businesses

Here is how to grow your business economically

Marketing when you do not have a big budget can be a challenge, but there is plenty a small business owner can do to attract and maintain a customer base. The rise in digital marketing has made it all the easier for the small business owner to find a way to create a presence and attract an informed buyer.

Before your business starts marketing a product, it helps to create a buyer persona whom you want to reach with your promotional materials. Once you have your ideal customer, you will have a wide choice of marketing methods. Most of these are low-cost or no-cost tactics (sometimes called guerrilla marketing). You may use different ones at various stages of your business cycle—or you may utilize them all at once from your business' inception.

When you build a business, the first thing you want to secure is a customer base. With a decent printer, a phone, and an internet-connected device, you can put together an extensive advertising campaign without having to pay for space. We will look at seven of these small business marketing techniques in more detail.

Key Takeaways

- Small businesses do not have the advertising budget of larger rivals, but there are plenty of inexpensive ways to build a customer base.

- Hitting the pavement with flyers distributed door to door (where allowed) and placing posters strategically can help get the word out.

- Follow up with customers after the first round of ads to reinforce the initial message. Do not fear cold calls—they can be effective.

- Value additions, such as discounts or freebies for repeat customers, are a big boon once the business is up and running.

- Referrals—both from customer to customer and business to business—are important as well.

- Prioritize digital marketing, including traditional websites and social media.

1. Flyers

This is the carpet-bombing method of cheap advertising. You find an area where you would like to do business and distribute flyers to all the mailboxes within reach. Your flyer should be brief and to the point, highlighting the services you offer or products you sell and providing contact information. Offering a free appraisal, coupon, or discount never hurts.

2. Posters

Most supermarkets, public spaces, and malls offer free bulletin board space for announcements and advertisements. This is a haphazard method, but you should try to make your poster visible and have removable tabs that the customers can present for a discount. Make each location an assorted color, so that you can get an idea from the tabs where the most leads are being generated. If one area is producing most of your leads, you can better target your campaign (flyers, ads in local media catering to those areas, cold calling, etc.)

3. Value Additions

This is one of the most powerful selling points for any product or service. On the surface, value additions are remarkably like coupons and free appraisals, but they are aimed at increasing customer satisfaction and widening the gap between you and the competition.

Common value additions include guarantees, discounts for repeat customers, point cards, and referral rewards. Often the deciding factor for a person picking between one of two similar shops is which shop has a point card or preferred customer card. You do not have to promise the moon to add value; you just must state something that the customer may not realize about your product or service. When you are making your advertising materials, the value additions should be highlighted.

4. Referral Networks

Referral networks are invaluable to a business. This does not only mean customer referrals, which are encouraged through discounts or other rewards per referral. This includes business-to-business referrals. If you have ever found yourself saying, "We don't do/sell that here, but X down the street does," you should make certain that you are getting a referral in return.

When dealing with white-collar professions, this network is even stronger. A lawyer refers people to an accountant, an accountant refers people to a broker, a financial planner refers people to a real estate agent. In each of these situations, the person stakes their professional reputation on the referral. Regardless of your business, make sure you create a referral network that has the same outlook and commitment to quality that you do.

As a final note on referral networks, remember that your competition is not always your enemy. If you are too busy to take a job, throw it their way. Most times you will find the favor returned. Besides, it can be bad for your reputation if a customer must wait too long.

5. Follow-Ups

Advertising can help you get a job, but what you do after a job can often be a much stronger marketing tool. Follow-up questionnaires are one of the best sources of feedback on how your ad campaign is going.

- Why did the customer choose your business?

- Where did they hear about it?

- Which other companies had they considered?

- What was the customer most satisfied with?

- What was the least satisfying?

Also, if your job involves going to the customer, make sure to slip a flyer into nearby mailboxes, as people of similar needs and interests tend to live in the same area.

6. Cold Calls

Unpleasant? Yes. Important? Yes.

Cold calling—whether it happens over the phone or door to door—is a baptism of fire for many small businesses. Cold calling forces you to sell yourself as well as your business. If people cannot buy you (the person talking to them), then they will not buy anything from you. Over the phone you do not have the benefit of a smile or face-to-face conversation—a phone is a license for people to be as caustic and abrupt as possible (we are all guilty of this at one time or another). However, cold calling does make you think on your feet and encourages creativity and adaptability when facing potential customers.

A combination of old-fashioned walking the streets and modern-day pounding the keyboard will provide the best results for a small business looking to market itself.

7. The Internet

It is difficult to overstate the internet's importance to building a successful business. Methods of marketing have stayed the same across the last 50 years, except for the birth and rapid evolution of the internet. No company (even a local café) should be without, at the very least, a website with vital details such as location and hours. You need a point of access for everyone who Googles first when they want to make a buying decision.

You also need a social media presence (Facebook page, Instagram, and Twitter accounts) combined with a content management system (CMS) with good search engine optimization (SEO). All this digital dexterity may feel intimidating at first. However, publishing technology has evolved to the point where WordPress—just one example of a free CMS—can meet all these needs. Yes, the internet is a beast. Make it your friendly one.

Ask yourself what are the 5 Biggest Challenges Facing Your Small Business

The Bottom Line

More than likely, you will find that the conversion rate on marketing is exceptionally low. Even the most successful campaigns measure leads (and converted sales from those leads) in the 10% to 20% range. This helps to shatter any illusions about instant success, but it is also an opportunity for improvement.

Do you want a company to buy your product? Give a presentation showing its benefits to that company. Do you want someone to use your service? Give an estimate or a sample of what you will do for them. Be confident, creative, and unapologetic, and people will eventually respond.

Small Business Is All About Relationships

It is not just whom you know, but how well you know them

With the world of business becoming increasingly more complex, small-business owners will find it extremely difficult to be an expert in all the specialized disciplines their businesses need. Despite the relentless requirement for small-business owners to generate and manage cash flow while bringing customers in the door, it is also critically important for them to cultivate business relationships with a reliable support team.

Key Takeaways

- Cultivating business relationships with outside providers of expertise is crucial to the success of a small business.

- Good employee and customer relationships are of primary importance.

- Necessary professionals include bankers, accountants, lawyers, insurance representatives, marketeers, specific skills trainers, and technology consultants.

Business Support Team Members

Depending on the nature of the business, its support group includes customers, employees, bankers, accountant/tax specialists, lawyers, insurance representatives, sales/marketing professionals, skills trainers, and technology consultants. As it is unlikely that all this expertise will be available in-house, it is crucial for owners to develop and maintain close working relationships with many of these outside providers before any emergency need arises. Here is a look at how cultivating relationships with each of these groups can favorably impact a small business.

Employees

The financial duties of a business owner begin with their relationship with their employees. It is the most important one to cultivate. Good employees represent a major resource in a small business, so the time and effort the owner invests in nurturing those relationships have a huge return on investment (ROI). Employees who feel respected, listened to, and appreciated by management produce at higher levels.

In addition, employees represent the company to its customers. The business relationship with customers depends on their experience and interaction with the firm's employees. Happy employees tend to want to satisfy the customers, do an excellent job, and work hard to retain that job. This is important to the continuity of high-quality customer service and avoids the significant expense of employee turnover, retraining, and the inevitable newcomer mistakes of new, inexperienced employees. Having trusted long-term employees can also free up the owner to handle offsite duties as needed.

Bankers

A banking relationship is an obvious need—not only for routine business banking but also for growing capital, increasing inventory, buying a building, bridging a short-term gap between payables and receivables, or addressing the seasonality of the cash flow in the business. The banker to whom an owner goes for a loan should know the business owner, understand the history of the business, and understand the owner's judgment and credibility regarding the reason for and ability to pay back the loan.

If the long-term relationship is there, or is at least in the process of being built, the loan request has a much better chance of being approved. If the business has borrowed and repaid loans in the past, the established history and relationship enhance the prospects of being approved.

Many small businesses try to find an accountant who can also double as their tax specialist to save time and money.

Accountant and Tax Specialist

A relationship with an accountant is equally important if the business owner is to be confident in the quality, clarity, timeliness, and understanding of the financial reporting provided. A relationship with an accountant can also enhance the business' credibility with a banker when seeking additional capital.

Many small businesses combine the accountant and tax-specialist functions in one outside entity for reasons of convenience, time saving, and cost. This may be advantageous if the accountant has broad tax experience for the relevant industry and expertise in tax management for the specific business the accounting firm serves.

Legal Professional

Every business owner should have a relationship with a business lawyer, liability attorney, or legal firm. When an owner invests money and effort in building a business, it must be safeguarded from loss that arises from a lawsuit. While it is important to collaborate with an attorney whom you can trust, it is also critical to choose one with experience in law for which you require their services.

Insurance Representative

As part of its risk management, a business should have a relationship with and seek out the trusted advice of an insurance representative. This professional should help provide the optimal levels of coverage in the areas of needed protection, keeping in mind any budgetary constraints.

Marketing Professional

Depending on the owner's sales and marketing expertise, a relationship with a marketing professional is highly advised. Most small businesses start with an entrepreneur who has a specific technical skill, trade certification, or loyal customers for excellent work done. When the owner wants to grow the business beyond the established customer base, they should have a well-defined marketing plan that addresses the following issues:

- ☐ Targeting the market

- ☐ Optimizing the media used in marketing efforts

- ☐ Creating a brand strategy

- ☐ Assessing the competition

- ☐ Getting the best value for any marketing money spent

Business Trainer

It is often the case that the owner and the employees need training. In a small business, especially in a startup, the owner may not have had time to acquire the types of skills necessary for managing a growing business with more employees, constantly evolving digital tools and systems, enlarging inventory, acquiring additional vehicles or equipment, and managing more customers. A relationship with an independent business-skills trainer can fill that need.

IT Specialist

A more recent arrival on the required-relationship list is the enterprise systems or information technology (IT) specialist. The business owner should have someone who can come in to analyze the existing digital systems and suggest ways to effectively and efficiently manage costs and optimize processes. That person (or organization) should suggest specific strategies to keep the business competitive in terms of administrative, project management, and operating costs while ensuring the scalability of the business model through process improvements, enhanced system capacity, flexibility, and information security best practices.

The Bottom Line

The importance of connections between people in business cannot be overstated. While these relationships can be many, they are not necessarily time-consuming. They are, however, essential to long-term business success and worth their weight in gold when the business needs experts to help solve problems or take full advantage of a business window of opportunity.

Balance Sheet vs. Profit and Loss Statement: What is the Difference?

Both involve a company's finances, but their differences are significant

The balance sheet and the profit and loss (P&L) statement are two of the three financial statements companies issue regularly. Such statements provide an ongoing record of a company's financial condition and are used by creditors, market analysts and investors to evaluate a company's financial soundness and growth potential. The third financial statement is called the cash-flow statement.

Key Takeaways

- A balance sheet reports a company's assets, liabilities, and shareholder equity at a specific point in time.

- A balance sheet provides both investors and creditors with a snapshot as to how effectively a company's management uses its resources.

- A profit and loss (P&L) statement summarizes the revenues, costs and expenses incurred during a specific period.

- A P&L statement provides information about whether a company can generate profit by increasing revenue, reducing costs, or both.

Balance Sheet

A balance sheet reports a company's assets, liabilities, and shareholder equity at a specific point in time. It provides a basis for computing rates of return and evaluating the company's capital structure. This financial statement provides a snapshot of what a company owns and owes, as well as the amount invested by shareholders.

The balance sheet shows a company's resources or assets, and it also shows how those assets are financed—whether through debt under liabilities or by issuing equity as shown in shareholder equity. The balance sheet provides both investors and creditors with a snapshot of how effectively a company's management uses its resources. Just like the other financial statements, the balance sheet is used to conduct financial analysis and to calculate financial ratios. Below are a few examples of the items on a typical balance sheet.

Assets

☐ Cash and Cash Equivalents. These are the most liquid assets, which may include Treasury bills (T-bills), short-term certificates of deposit (CDs) and cash.

☐ Marketable Securities. This category includes equity and debt securities for which there is a liquid market.

☐ Receivables. Also known as accounts receivable, this represents money owed to the company by customers.

☐ Inventory. This area covers all the goods available for sale.

Liabilities

☐ Debt. This includes the current portion of long-term debt and bank indebtedness.

☐ Overhead. This accounts for such financial obligations as rent, tax, and utilities.

☐ Payables. This includes both wages and dividends owed.

Shareholder Equity

Shareholder equity is equal to a firm's total assets minus its total liabilities and is one of the most common financial metrics employed by analysts to determine the financial health of a company. Shareholder equity represents the net value of a company, meaning the amount that would be returned to shareholders if all the company's assets were liquidated and all its debts repaid.

Retained earnings are recorded under shareholder equity and refer to the percentage of net earnings not paid out as dividends but retained by the company either to be reinvested in its core business or to pay the debt.

Trial Balance vs. the Balance Sheet

It is important to note that the trial balance is different from the balance sheet. This is an internal report that stays in the accounting department. The balance sheet, on the other hand, is a financial statement distributed to other departments, investors, and lenders.

The trial balance provides financial information at the account level, such as general ledger accounts, and is therefore more granular. Eventually, the information in the trial balance is used to prepare the financial statements for the period.

In contrast, the balance sheet aggregates multiple accounts, summing up the number of assets, liabilities, and shareholder equity in the accounting records at a specific time. The balance sheet includes outstanding expenses, accrued income, and the value of the closing stock, whereas the trial balance does not. In addition, the balance sheet must adhere to a standard format as described in an accounting framework, such as the International Financial Reporting Standards (IFRS) or the accepted accounting principles (GAAP).

Profit and Loss (P&L) Statement

A P&L statement, often referred to as the income statement, is a financial statement that summarizes the revenues, costs, and expenses incurred during a specific period, usually a fiscal year or quarter. These records provide information about a company's ability (or lack thereof) to generate profit by increasing revenue, reducing costs, or both. The P&L statement's many monikers include the "statement of profit and loss," the "statement of operations," the "statement of financial results," and the "income and expense statement."

Top Line and Bottom Line

The P&L statement provides the top and bottom line for a company. It begins with an entry for revenue, known as the top line, and subtracts the costs of doing business, including the cost of goods sold, operating expenses, tax expenses, interest expenses, and any other expenses sometimes referred to as "extraordinary" or "one-time" expenses. The difference, known as the bottom line, is net income, also referred to as profit or earnings.

Realized Profits and Loss

The P&L statement reveals the company's realized profits or losses for the specified period by comparing total revenues to the company's total costs and expenses. Over time it can show a company's ability to increase its profit, either by reducing costs and expenses or increasing sales. Companies publish P&L statements annually, at the end of the company's fiscal year, and may also publish them on a quarterly basis. Accountants, analysts, and investors study a P&L statement carefully, scrutinizing cash flow and debt financing capabilities.

Revenues and Expenses

From an accounting standpoint, revenues and expenses are listed on the P&L statement when they are incurred, not when the money flows in or out. One beneficial aspect of the P&L statement is that it uses operating and nonoperating revenues and expenses, as defined by the Internal Revenue Service (IRS) and GAAP.

A balance sheet considers a specific point in time, while a P&L statement is concerned with a set period.

Balance Sheet vs. P&L Statement

Although the balance sheet and the P&L statement contain some of the same financial information—including revenues, expenses, and profits—there are significant differences between them. Here is the main one: The balance sheet reports the assets, liabilities, and shareholder equity at a specific point in time, while a P&L statement summarizes a company's revenues, costs, and expenses during a specific period.

Purpose of Each Statement

Each document is built for a slightly different purpose. Balance sheets are built more broadly, revealing what the company owns and owes as well as any long-term investments. Unlike an income statement, the full value of long-term investments or debts appears on the balance sheet. The name "balance sheet" is derived from the way that the three major accounts eventually balance out and equal each other. All assets are listed in one section, and their sum must equal the sum of all liabilities and the shareholder equity.

The P&L statement answers an extremely specific question: Is the company profitable? While accountants use the P&L statement to help gauge the accuracy of financial transactions—and investors use the P&L statement to judge a company's health—the company itself can review its own statement for productive purposes. Closely monitoring financial statements highlights where revenue is strong and where expenses are incurred efficiently, and the opposite is true as well. For example, a company might notice increasing sales but decreasing profits and search for innovative solutions to reduce costs of operation.

Profit vs. Total Value

The P&L statement shows net income, meaning whether a company is in the red or black. The balance sheet shows how much a company is worth, meaning its total value. Though both are a little oversimplified, this is often how the P&L statement and the balance sheet tend to be interpreted by investors and lenders.

It is important to note that investors should be careful to not confuse earnings/profits with cash flow. It is possible for a firm to operate profitably without generating cash flow or to generate cash flow without producing profits.

How the Statements Are Calculated

The P&L statement requires accountants to add up the company's revenue on one portion and add up all its expenses on another. The total amount of expenses is subtracted from the total revenue, resulting in a profit or loss. The balance sheet has a few different calculations that are all performed as representations of one basic formula:

Assets = Liabilities + Owner's Equity

The Bottom Line

When used together along with other financial documents, the balance sheet and P&L statement can be used to assess the operational efficiency, year-to-year consistency, and organizational direction of a company. For this reason, the numbers reported in each document are scrutinized by investors and the company's executives. While the presentation of these statements varies slightly from industry to industry, large discrepancies between the annual treatment of either document are often considered a red flag.

A firm's ability (or inability) to generate earnings consistently over time is a major driver of stock prices and bond valuations. For this reason, every investor should be curious about all the financial statements—including the P&L statement and the balance sheet—of any company of interest. Once reviewed as a group, these financial statements should then be compared with those of other companies in the industry to obtain performance benchmarks and understand any potential market-wide trends.

Lines of Credit: The Basics

This lesser-known loan option can work well under the right circumstances

When individuals need money, seeking a line of credit is often the last thing that occurs to them. What comes to mind first is going to a bank for a traditional fixed- or variable-rate loan, using credit cards, borrowing from friends or family, or turning to specialized peer-to-peer or social lending or donation sites on the web. In the direst of circumstances, there are pawnshops or payday lenders.

Businesses have been using credit lines for years to meet working capital needs and/or take advantage of strategic investment opportunities, but they've never quite caught on as much with individuals. Some of this may be since banks often do not advertise lines of credit, and potential borrowers do not think to ask. The only credit line borrowing that might come up is a home equity line of credit or HELOC. But that is a loan secured by the borrower's home, with its own issues and risks.

Here, then, are some of the basics about lines of credit.

Key Takeaways

- A line of credit is a flexible loan from a financial institution that consists of a defined amount of money that you can access as needed and repay either immediately or over time.

- Interest is charged on a line of credit as soon as money is borrowed.

- Lines of credit are most often used to cover the gaps in irregular monthly income or finance a project whose cost cannot be predicted up front.

What Is a Line of Credit?

A line of credit is a flexible loan from a bank or financial institution. Like a credit card that offers you a limited amount of funds—funds that you can use when, if, and how you wish—a line of credit is a defined amount of money that you can access as needed and then repay immediately or over a prespecified period. As with a loan, a line of credit will charge interest as soon as money is borrowed, and borrowers must be approved by the bank, with such approval a byproduct of the borrower's credit rating and/or relationship with the bank. Note that the interest rate is variable, which makes it difficult to predict what the money you borrow will end up costing you.

Lines of credit tend to be lower-risk revenue sources relative to credit card loans, but they do complicate a bank's earning asset management, as the outstanding balances can't really be controlled once the line of credit has been approved. They address the fact that banks are not terribly interested in underwriting one-time personal loans, particularly unsecured loans, for most customers. Likewise, it is not economical for a borrower to take out a loan every month or two, repay it, and then borrow again. Lines of credit answer both issues by making a specified amount of money available when the borrower needs it.

How Line of Credit Works

When a Line of Credit Is Useful

Lines of credit are not intended to be used to fund one-time purchases such as houses or cars—which is what mortgages and auto loans are for, respectively—though lines of credit can be used to acquire items for which a bank might not normally underwrite a loan. Most commonly, individual lines of credit are intended for the same basic purpose as business lines of credit: to smooth out the vagaries of variable monthly income and expenses or to finance projects where it may be difficult to ascertain the exact funds needed in advance.

Consider a self-employed person whose monthly income is irregular or who experiences a significant, often unpredictable delay between performing the work and collecting the pay. While said person might usually rely on credit cards to deal with the cash-flow crunches, a line of credit can be a cheaper option (it typically offers lower interest rates) and offer more-flexible repayment schedules. Lines of credit can also help fund estimated quarterly tax payments, particularly when there is a discrepancy between the timing of the "accounting profit" and the actual receipt of cash.

In short, lines of credit can be useful in situations where there will be repeated cash outlays, but the amounts may not be known upfront and/or the vendors may not accept credit cards, and in situations that require large cash deposits—weddings being one good example. Likewise, lines of credit were often quite popular during the housing boom to fund home improvement or refurbishment projects. People would frequently get a mortgage to buy the dwelling and simultaneously obtain a line of credit to help fund whatever renovations or repairs were needed.

Personal lines of credit have also appeared as part of bank-offered overdraft protection plans. While not all banks are particularly eager to explain overdraft protection as a loan product ("It's a service, not a loan!"), and not all overdraft protection plans are underpinned by personal lines of credit, many are. Here again, though, is an example of the use of a line of credit as a source of emergency funds on a quick, as-needed basis.

There is always a credit evaluation process when you apply to a bank for a line of credit.

The Problems with Lines of Credit

Like any loan product, lines of credit are potentially both useful and dangerous. If investors do tap a line of credit, that money must be paid back (and the terms for such paybacks are spelled out at the time when the line of credit is initially granted). Accordingly, there is a credit evaluation process, and would-be borrowers with poor credit will have a much harder time being approved.

Likewise, it is not free money. Unsecured lines of credit—that is, lines of credit not tied to the equity in your home or some other valuable property—are certainly cheaper than loans from pawnshops or payday lenders and usually cheaper than credit cards, but they're more expensive than traditional secured loans, such as mortgages or auto loans. In most cases the interest on a line of credit is not tax deductible.

Some banks will charge a maintenance fee (either monthly or annually) if you do not use the line of credit, and interest starts accumulating as soon as money is borrowed. Because lines of credit can be drawn on and repaid on an unscheduled basis, some borrowers may find the interest calculations for lines of credit more complicated and be surprised at what they end up paying in interest.

Comparing Lines of Credit to Other Types of Borrowing

As suggested above, there are many similarities between lines of credit and other financing methods, but there are also significant differences that borrowers need to understand.

Credit Cards

Like credit cards, lines of credit effectively have preset limits—you are approved to borrow a certain amount of money and no more. Also, like credit cards, policies for going over that limit vary with the lender, though banks tend to be less willing than credit cards to immediately approve overages (instead, they often look to renegotiate the line of credit and increase the borrowing limit). Again, as with plastic, the loan is preapproved, and the money can be accessed whenever the borrower wants, for whatever use. Lastly, while credit cards and lines of credit may have annual fees, neither charge interest until there is an outstanding balance.

Unlike credit cards, lines of credit can be secured with real property. Prior to the housing crash, home equity lines of credit (HELOCs) were extremely popular with both lending officers and borrowers. While HELOCs are harder to get now, they are still available and tend to carry lower interest rates. Credit cards will always have minimum monthly payments, and companies will significantly increase the interest rate if those payments are not met. Lines of credit may or may not have similar immediate monthly repayment requirements.

Loans

Like a traditional loan, a line of credit requires acceptable credit and repayment of the funds and charges interest on any funds borrowed. Also like a loan, taking out, using, and repaying a line of credit can improve a borrower's credit score.

Unlike a loan, which is for a fixed amount for a fixed time with a prearranged repayment schedule, a line of credit has both more flexibility and a variable rate of interest. When interest rates rise, your line of credit will cost more, not the case with a loan at fixed interest. There are also typically fewer restrictions on the use of funds borrowed under a line of credit. A mortgage must go toward the purchase of the listed property, and an auto loan must go toward the specified car, but a line of credit can be used at the discretion of the borrower.

If you decide that a loan is best for you, finding the best place to borrow can be particularly stressful when you face a financial emergency and you need money in a hurry. For those with the additional obstacle of less-than-stellar credit, accessing cash quickly may seem even more daunting. Fortunately, there are a variety of emergency loan options that may be available to you even when you have credit problems.

Payday and Pawn Loans

There are some superficial similarities between lines of credit and payday and pawn loans, but that is only since many payday or pawn loan borrowers are "frequent flyers" who repeatedly borrow, repay, or extend their loans (paying extremely high fees and interest along the way). Likewise, a pawnbroker or payday lender does not care what a borrower uses the funds for, so long as the loan is repaid, and all its fees are remitted.

The differences, however, are considerable. For anyone who can qualify for a line of credit, the cost of funds will be dramatically lower than for a payday or pawn loan. Similarly, the credit evaluation process is much simpler and less demanding for a payday or pawn loan (there may be no credit check at all), and you get your funds much, much more quickly. It is also the case that payday lenders and pawnbrokers seldom offer the amounts of money often approved in lines of credit. And on their side, banks seldom bother with lines of credit as small as the average payday or pawn loan.

The Bottom Line

Lines of credit are like any financial product—neither inherently good nor bad. It is all in how people use them. On one hand, excessive borrowing against a line of credit can get somebody into financial trouble just as surely as spending with credit cards. On the other hand, lines of credit can be cost-effective solutions to month-to-month financial vagaries or executing a complicated transaction such as a wedding or home remodeling. As is the case with any loan, borrowers should pay careful attention to the terms (particularly the fees, interest rate, and repayment schedule), shop around, and not be afraid to ask plenty of questions before signing.

Using a Business Credit Card

They are known for their ease and convenience, but there are pitfalls

What Is a Business Credit Card?

If you are a small business owner, you have received numerous offers and applications for a small business credit card. It can be a convenient way to increase your company's purchasing power.

Small business credit cards provide business owners with easy access to a revolving line of credit with a set credit limit to make purchases and withdraw cash. Like a consumer credit card, a small business credit card carries an interest charge if the balance is not repaid in full each billing cycle. You may be able to get a credit card through your bank or apply online. You can compare card terms and features through Investopedia's best business credit cards roundup review or by consulting our reviews of individual credit cards, which always include a section comparing the card being reviewed to several other cards.

A business credit card can be a convenient way to quickly access financing for short-term needs and increase your company's purchasing power. It is often marketed as an attractive alternative to a traditional line of credit. Like any source of financing, a business credit card comes at a cost and must be carefully managed.

Key Takeaways

- A business credit card gives small business owners easy access to a revolving line of credit with a set limit.

- It has an interest charge if the balance is not repaid in full each business cycle.

- Said interest rate is usually much higher than the rate on a small business loan.

- A small business owner decides which employees may have a business credit card.

How a Business Credit Card Works

Without a good system in place, it can be difficult to keep track of—and keep a handle on—credit card spending, which affects your bottom line. Certain strategies can be utilized to ensure good credit card practices.

Ensuring Accountability

"The most key step a small business can take to make sure credit cards are used effectively is to set up a bomb-proof accountability system," says John Burton, founding partner of Moon shadow Leadership Solutions in Bryson City, N.C. "This could mean everything from preapproval of all credit card spending to rigorous requiring of receipts to pulling credit cards from those who do not report completely and on time with receipts," says Burton. Have a system in place before the first credit card arrives and, Burton says, be consistent, rigorous, and fair while tolerating no exceptions.

Deciding Who Receives a Card

Burton acknowledges the challenges employers may face in deciding who gets a credit card. "I've seen businesses that lost control of credit card spending by issuing too many cards to too many people and thinking that all important officers and travelers needed the convenience of a company credit card," says Burton. While giving everyone a credit card might seem like the right or easy thing to do, it can lead to a "dysfunctional, expensive system and a serious lack of control and accountability," he explains.

Use alternatives and establish rules. "Many companies, especially with salespeople, reimburse for company spending on personal credit cards with excellent accountability—i.e., no receipt, no reimbursement," says Burton. It is helpful, however, to have clear rules regarding who gets a card, whether it is based on seniority, position, or other factors. This can help avoid confusion and mitigate bad feelings from employees who would like a card but are not eligible.

Setting Credit Card Limits

Every business should have clear policies about spending, including which expenses can be put on cards, how much employees can spend, and how often they can use their cards. It is important to put the policy in writing and have every employee who is issued a card read and sign it. After they do, give each cardholder a copy to use for reference.

Depending on the business card, you may be able to set up restrictions that limit transactions to a certain dollar amount, spending category, and even certain days and times. With some cards you can set up individual restrictions for each employee. For example, you may limit one employee to $50 a day any day of the week for gas purchases, while limiting another to $100 for gas and $50 for meals each day, but only on business days.

Being Watchful of Card Activity

Many business credit cards allow you to set up activity alerts that arrive as text or email messages. The alerts can be set up to notify you each time a transaction takes place or only if an employee uses (or tries to use) a card in an unapproved manner. You can also take advantage of online and mobile banking to view up-to-the-minute account activity. Your accounting department should review each statement to make sure each line item is a charge you authorized.

Using a business credit card for large purchases that cannot be fully paid for before the interest charges kick in can prove an expensive proposition.

Using the Card Wisely

It is important to know when a business should use credit. It is not always the best choice, especially for large expenditures that cannot be paid in full before interest kicks in. Even though it takes extra effort to secure a loan from a bank or other lending institution, it often makes financial sense to do so, as the interest rate on credit cards is typically much higher than for such secured debt instruments. It's also possible that a large purchase—or a couple of large expenditures—can max out your credit card and leave you without a source of funds at all.

Pros

- Easier to qualify for a card than for a loan

- Convenience

- Provides a financial cushion

- Useful online

- Helps with bookkeeping

- Rewards and incentives

- Tool to build credit

Cons

- More expensive than a loan or credit line

- Personal legal liability

- Security issues

- Less protection than consumer credit cards offer

- Fluctuating interest rates

Business Credit Card Benefits

Along with providing the necessary cash flow to help maintain and build your business, credit cards can offer these advantages:

- **Easier Qualification**—It can be easier for business owners who do not have a well-established credit history to qualify for a revolving line of credit with a credit card, especially if it's secured, rather than a traditional line of credit or bank loan.

- **Convenience**—Credit cards are the ultimate in financing convenience. Business owners can access funds for purchases or cash withdrawal much more quickly and easily than having to find cash and/or use a checkbook.

- **Financial Cushion**—A credit card can provide business owners with a much-needed financial cushion when accounts receivable are behind or sales are slow, and the business is short on cash.

- **Online Ease**—Increasingly, business owners make purchases and do business online with vendors, contractors, and suppliers. Using a credit card makes online transactions easier.

- **Bookkeeping Assistance**—In addition to receiving a monthly statement, most cards provide small business card holders with online record-keeping tools to manage their accounts, including a year-end account summary, which can help a bookkeeper track, categorize, and manage expenses. It can simplify bookkeeping, help when using outside professionals to navigate an audit and pay taxes, and provide a straightforward way to monitor employee spending.

- **Rewards and Incentives**—Many cards offer business owners rewards programs—including airline miles and shopping discounts—for using the card. Some also provide cash back incentives, repaying cardholders a percentage of their purchases. In short, it can pay to choose carefully, so that you receive the best rewards card possible for your need.

- **A Tool to Build Credit**—Responsibly using a small business credit card—which means paying the bill on time, paying more than the minimum due, and not going over the credit limit (which can trigger an over-limit fee)—can be a straightforward way to build up a positive credit report for your business. That, in turn, can help you be more likely to qualify for a loan or line of credit, and at a potentially lower interest rate, in the future. Keep in mind that irresponsible use of a business credit card can damage your credit, however.

A business credit card can be used as a credit-building tool, allowing your company to qualify for other, less costly financial help, such as a small business loan.

Business Credit Card Disadvantages

Before rushing to apply for a business credit card, it is important to consider these potential downsides:

- **More Expensive**—The convenience and ease of small business credit cards come at a price, as they typically charge a much higher interest rate than a small business loan or fixed line of credit offered by a bank. That interest can add up quickly if card activity is not repaid on time and in full each month. In addition—without a system to regularly and carefully monitor card usage—it can be easy to accidentally overextend your firm financially by going over its credit limit or incurring late fees and penalties.

- **Personal Legal Liability**—Many small business credit cards require a personal-liability agreement (your personal security) to repay debt. This means that any late or missed payment could result in a negative personal credit report and the inability to personally borrow money. You also may have to pay more with a higher interest rate.

- **Security Issues**—Security measures should be created to ensure that cards or card information are not stolen by employees, vendors, contractors, and others who come through the office space. It's also important to make sure that employees who are authorized to use the card do not use them for personal spending, and that they take precautions when making online transactions to avoid being hacked.

- **Less Protection**—Small business credit cards often do not carry the same protection as consumer credit cards. For example, many cards will not provide the same level of assured services when disputing billing errors or needing to make merchandise returns. Be sure to review the level of protection and services a card offers before applying.

- **Fluctuating Interest Rates**—Unlike with a loan or fixed line of credit, the company that issues your credit card can reset its interest rate depending on how you use and manage your account.3 As such, it can pay to be aware of how rates work and can change.

The Cost of Hiring a New Employee

You need to figure in recruitment, training, benefits, and more

Cash-strapped businesses often hesitate to start hiring, even when they need workers, due to the actual cost of hiring employees. It's easy to forget that the cost of taking on a new employee means more than just their salary, which can be substantial all by itself. But once you factor in the cost of recruiting, training, and more, the dollars start adding up. In its 2016 Human Capital Benchmarking Report, the Society for Human Resource Management estimated that companies spend an average of 42 days to fill a position and $4,129 per hire.

Key Takeaways

- The cost of hiring an employee goes far beyond just paying for their salary to encompass recruiting, training, benefits, and more.

- Small companies spent, on average, more than $1,500 on training, per employee, in 2019.

- Integrating a new employee into the organization can also require time and expenditures.

- It can take up to six months or more for a company to break even on its investment in a new hire.

The Cost of Hiring A New Employee

The Cost of Recruiting

Just the price of finding the right person to hire can be hefty. There are various potentially excessive costs just in the process of recruiting, according to business consultant Bill Bliss, president of Bliss & Associates Inc. These include advertising the opening, the time cost of an internal recruiter, the time cost of a recruiter's assistant in reviewing resumes and performing other recruitment-related tasks, the time cost of the person conducting the interviews, drug screens and background checks, and various pre-employment assessment tests.

Not every new hire will require the same process, but even an $8/hour employee can end up costing a company around $3,500 in turnover costs, both direct and indirect.

The Cost of Training

Recruitment is just the first step in the process. Once the right person is in place, businesses need to provide adequate training so the new employee can do the work and start producing for the company. Training turns out to be one of the costliest investments a company can make.

According to a recent study by Training Magazine, companies spent an average of $1,286 a year on training per employee in 2019. During the same year, employees devoted an average of 42.1 hours to training. And those are not necessarily only new hires who would not only require the same on-the-job training and continuing education as current employees, but the additional hours, cost of orientation, and initial job training as well.

Entrepreneur and consultant Scott Allen provides a straightforward way to understand training cost: "Calculate the cost of both structured training (including materials) and the time of managers and key coworkers to train the new employee to the point of 100% productivity."5

The Cost of Salary and Benefits

The obvious cost of a new employee—the salary—comes with its own bundle of side items. Benefits range from the minor, such as free coffee in the employee break room, to the major, such as life insurance, disability coverage, medical and dental plans, tuition reimbursement... the list goes on. According to Joe Hadzima, a columnist for the Boston Business Journal and senior lecturer at MIT's Sloan School of Management, the salary plus benefits usually totals "in the 1.25 to 1.4 times base salary range." Hence, the salary-plus-benefits package for an employee who makes $50,000 a year could equal $62,500 to $70,000.

The Cost of Workplace Integration

Another minor point should not be overlooked: Workplace integration, from assigning the new hire a desk to placing them with the right team of peers, can be costly. Businesses are looking at more than simply providing a computer and an ergonomically designed desk chair; there is also the cost of physical space as well as software, cell phone, travel, and any special equipment or resources required for the job.

Expenditures may also change because of adaptations required for the safety of office workers returning during the pandemic. Many of these are in the process of being explored now.

The Break-Even Point

The goal of all this investment is increased productivity—at least that's why businesses make the investment. But it can take time for the costs to get covered and companies to see a return on their investment. A survey of 210 CEOs by Harvard Business School estimates that typical mid-level managers require 6 months to reach their breakeven point (BEP). In other words, a mid-level manager must be on the job for more than six months for the company to earn back its investment on that hire.

Bliss breaks down the productivity scale into three periods:

- **The first month:** After training is completed, new employees are functioning at about 25% productivity, which means that the cost of lost productivity is 75% of the employee's salary.

- **Weeks 5 through 8:** The level goes up to 50% productivity, with a corresponding cost of 50% of the employee's salary.

- **Weeks 9 through 12**: In this timeframe, the employee usually reaches a productivity rate of up to 75%, with the cost being 25% of the employee's salary.

- **Following the 12-week mark:** Companies can expect a new hire to reach full productivity.

The Bottom Line

Hiring a new employee is not a decision that should be taken lightly, as it does not fall lightly on the company budget. But without workers, there is not much work done, so even though the investment may make the company accountant cringe, the potential in return on a good new hire continues to make the investment worthwhile.

Raise vs. Bonus for Your Small Business Employees

How to reward your staff without harming your bottom line

Hiring and retaining top-tier talent is a key objective for business owners, and paying employees is an important part of the recipe for success. Employees are the backbone of every small business. They are the face of the enterprise and directly influence its success or failure.

Evaluating the pros and cons of raises versus bonuses—and striking the right balance between the two—can help a business owner achieve staffing goals while also maintaining a healthy bottom line or profits.

Key Takeaways

- Raises and bonuses boost morale, incentivize employees, and ensure that staff feel rewarded and appreciated.

- Raises are a permanent increase in payroll expenses; bonuses are a variable cost and therefore give business owners greater financial flexibility when business is down.

- Bonuses can be tied to sales or production volumes to incentivize employees and help companies boost their profits during peak times.

- Other forms of compensation include partnerships, stock, profit-sharing, and even tickets to cultural or sports events and gift certificates.

- Business owners need to gauge the effect of raises and/or bonuses on their company's profit margin.

Understanding The Right Compensation Mix

Most people go to work to make money. From an employee's perspective, more is better. However, employers may not always be able to pay their employees more. As a result, many small business owners offer employee compensation packages that are made up of a mix of salary raises and periodic bonuses. This type of compensation package gives an owner the flexibility to reward employees when business conditions are good and adjust variable costs to reduce expenses when business conditions are tough.

Raises

Some companies give out across-the-board raises each year, with every employee receiving the same amount. The raise could be a set percentage based on the employee's pay. An annual raise helps employees plan and budget for their monthly expenses by helping them keep up with the cost of living. Although there are many ways to motivate and retain a company's best employees, raises help boost employee morale and ensure that long-time employees are rewarded more than their new hires.

A small percentage raise each year can be less costly than paying bonuses that may fluctuate with sales or production numbers. However, annual raises are a permanent increase in the cost of doing business. Often, payroll is the largest expense for a company. As a result, it is important that business owners determine whether the company generates enough revenue and monthly cash flow to meet the increased payroll expenses.

Cash flow is the net amount of inflow and outflow of cash from a company and is reported on a cash flow statement. Business owners must include the increased salary expenses in their monthly budgets using their cash flow and revenue estimates. A cash-flow shortage could disrupt a business' day-to-day operations.

Companies with predictable and steadily rising profits might find it easier to issue raises than companies with periodic or seasonal earnings. Also, companies with variable costs and less-predictable revenues are typically more reluctant to impose a permanent increase in payroll expenses.

Bonuses

Bonuses can be more financially feasible for business owners to manage since they're a variable cost, with payment tied to sales or production volumes, for example. Bonuses incentivize employees to exhibit the behavior that a business needs to be successful, whether it is generating new clients, client retention, or improving cost controls. While pay raises typically reward longevity, bonuses are paid based on performance.

Since the compensation is variable, a bonus can be reduced or eliminated if business conditions make it difficult or impossible to fund them. The variable cost structure of a bonus package helps business owners during times of low sales or production volumes. Pay raises are permanent, but bonuses keep payroll costs lower when the revenue is not there to pay them.

While the ability to minimize or avoid the expense of bonuses is attractive for business owners, it can be detrimental to staff morale. Employees rely on their income to pay bills and put food on the table. Large, unpredictable fluctuations can be disruptive and cause workers to seek employment elsewhere. Because of this, employers need to communicate to staff members that the ability to reduce expenses, when necessary, not only helps the company save money but also avoids the need to make staff reductions when business temporarily slows. In a well-run business, cutting bonuses can save jobs.

How Big a Bonus and What Type?

A typical payout structure is 3% to 5% of annual salary for clerical and support staff. Managers might receive payments in the low double-digit percentage range, with executives in the mid-double-digit range. Senior executives at the highest levels may receive most of their compensation via bonus payments.

Bonuses can be structured to recognize individual merit or to reward collective success. Individual merit–based bonuses reward top-producing employees for their efforts.

Sales-based bonus, for example, could be paid to employees who generate the newest business. Production-based bonuses could be structured for those who answer the most customer phone calls or produce the most widgets.

Also, bonuses can be set up as a short-term incentive, say, for a new directive or sales campaign. A three-month sales initiative to bring in new business or a business with seasonal production increases, for example, could be tied to a bonus system.

By incentivizing employees during peak periods, a company can maximize its revenue and profits during a critical time of the year.

A bonus can also be based on the overall company's success. If the company hits its sales goals, profitability goals, or other defined metrics, all employees are rewarded. Under a company-based system, employees often receive a predetermined payment amount that is based on the collective achievements of the corporation rather than individual performance.

In short, bonuses can be part of an employee's ongoing compensation package or offered as one-time events to recognize significant milestones such as growth, profitability, or longevity.

Other Forms of Compensation

While cash bonuses are the most familiar form of a bonus, there are other forms that may be worth considering. Companies can offer an ownership stake in the company, which can come in the form of a partnership offer in the firm, or through shares of stock. Smaller companies that cannot extend such offers could consider the creation of a profit-sharing plan that makes a discretionary payment toward employees' retirement savings.

There are various unique employee offerings that can provide an incentive for team members. Possibilities include granting extra vacation days, awarding tickets to sporting or cultural events, or giving movie passes or gift certificates. These small tokens of appreciation are available to even the smallest businesses at a reasonable cost.

What is the Financial Impact on the Business?

It is also important to consider the impact of bonuses and raises on a company's profit margins. A company's margin is the amount of profit generated as a percentage of sales. If, for example, a company has a margin of 35%, it means the company generates thirty-five cents for each dollar of sales. Business owners must analyze how a bonus versus a raise would impact their company's profit margin.

It can be helpful to back test a raise or bonus incentive plan with a prior year's financial performance to gauge how much expenses would rise and impact profit margins. Of course, it is difficult to estimate the increased number of sales that would have been generated had a bonus structure existed in prior years. However, applying a potential raise and bonus payout structure to prior years' sales and revenue figures should provide owners with a sense of the potential cash flow scenarios.

Since employees are at the heart of every business, rewarding them properly is critical to success—and to holding onto your best performers. Any compensation model should involve incentivizing employees and providing ongoing communication to ensure team members know their efforts are appreciated.

Outsourcing

What Is Outsourcing?

Outsourcing is the business practice of hiring a party outside a company to perform services or create goods that were traditionally performed in-house by the company's own employees and staff. Outsourcing is a practice usually undertaken by companies as a cost-cutting measure. As such, it can affect a wide range of jobs, ranging from customer support to manufacturing to the back office.

Outsourcing was first recognized as a business strategy in 1989 and became an integral part of business economics throughout the 1990s.1 The practice of outsourcing is subject to considerable controversy in many countries. Those opposed argue that it has caused the loss of domestic jobs, particularly in the manufacturing sector. Supporters say it creates an incentive for businesses and companies to allocate resources where they are most effective, and that outsourcing helps maintain the nature of free-market economies on a global scale.

Key Takeaways

- Companies use outsourcing to cut labor costs, including salaries for their personnel, overhead, equipment, and technology.

- Outsourcing is also used by companies to dial down and focus on the core aspects of the business, spinning off the less critical operations to outside organizations.

- On the downside, communication between the company and outside providers can be hard, and security threats can amp up when multiple parties can access sensitive data.

Outsourcing

Understanding Outsourcing

Outsourcing can help businesses reduce labor costs significantly. When a company uses outsourcing, it enlists the help of outside organizations not affiliated with the company to complete certain tasks. The outside organizations typically set up different compensation structures with their employees than the outsourcing company, enabling them to complete the work for less money. This enables the company that chose to outsource to lower its labor costs.

Businesses can also avoid expenses associated with overhead, equipment, and technology.

In addition to cost savings, companies can employ an outsourcing strategy to better focus on the core aspects of the business. Outsourcing non-core activities can improve efficiency and productivity because another entity performs these smaller tasks better than the firm itself. This strategy may also lead to faster turnaround times, increased competitiveness within an industry, and the cutting of overall operational costs.

Companies use outsourcing to cut labor costs and business expenses, but also to enable them to focus on the core aspects of the business.

Examples of Outsourcing

Outsourcing's biggest advantages are time and cost savings. A manufacturer of personal computers might buy internal components for its machines from other companies to save on production costs. A law firm might store and back up its files using a cloud-computing service provider, thus giving it access to digital technology without investing copious amounts of money to own the technology.

A small company may decide to outsource bookkeeping duties to an accounting firm, as doing so may be cheaper than retaining an in-house accountant. Other companies find outsourcing the functions of human resource departments, such as payroll and health insurance, as beneficial. When used properly, outsourcing is an effective strategy to reduce expenses, and can even provide a business with a competitive advantage over rivals.

Criticism of Outsourcing

Outsourcing does have disadvantages. Signing contracts with other companies may take time and extra effort from a firm's legal team. Security threats occur if another party has access to a company's confidential information and then that party suffers a data breach. A lack of communication between the company and the outsourced provider may occur, which could delay the completion of projects.

Special Considerations

Outsourcing internationally can help companies benefit from the differences in labor and production costs among countries. Price dispersion in another country may entice a business to relocate some or all its operations to the cheaper country to increase profitability and stay competitive within an industry. Many large corporations have eliminated their entire in-house customer service call centers, outsourcing that function to third-party outfits located in lower-cost locations.

What Is Outsourcing?

First seen as a formal business strategy in 1989, outsourcing is the process of hiring third parties to conduct services that were typically performed by the company. Often, outsourcing is used so that a company can focus on its core operations. It is also used to cut costs on labor, among others. While privacy has been a recent area of controversy for outsourcing contractors, it has also drawn criticism for its impact on the labor market in domestic economies.

What Is an Example of Outsourcing?

Consider a bank that outsources its customer service operations. Here, all customer-facing inquiries or complaints with concern to its online banking service would be handled by a third party. While choosing to outsource some business operations is often a complex decision, the bank determined that it would prove to be the most effective allocation of capital, given both consumer demand, the specialty of the third-party, and cost-saving attributes.

What Are the Disadvantages of Outsourcing?

The disadvantages of outsourcing include communication difficulties, security threats where sensitive data is increasingly at stake, and additional legal duties. On a broader level, outsourcing may have the potential to disrupt a labor force. One example that often comes to mind is the manufacturing industry in America, where now a considerable extent of production has moved internationally. In turn, higher-skilled manufacturing jobs, such as robotics or precision machines, have emerged at a greater scale.

Commercial Health Insurance

What Is Commercial Health Insurance?

Commercial health insurance is health insurance provided and administered by nongovernmental entities. It can cover medical expenses and disability income for the insured.

As of 2020, 1,096 health insurers filed statements with the National Association of Insurance Commissioners (NAIC), a nonprofit that sets standards for the U.S. insurance industry and provides support to insurance regulators.

Key Takeaways

- Nongovernmental agencies provide and administer what is called commercial health insurance.

- Two of the most popular types of commercial health insurance plans are the preferred provider organization (PPO) and health maintenance organization (HMO).

- Most commercial insurance is provided as group-sponsored insurance, offered by an employer.

- Although not administered by the government, plan offerings, to a large degree, are regulated and overseen by each state.

Understanding Commercial Health Insurance

Commercial health insurance policies are primarily sold by for-profit public and private carriers. Licensed agents and brokers sell plans to the public or group members; however, customers can also purchase directly from the carrier in many instances. These policies vary widely in the amount and types of specific coverage that they provide.

The term "commercial" distinguishes these types of policies from insurance that's provided by a public or government program, such as Medicaid, Medicare, or the State Children's Health Insurance Program (SCHIP). In broad terms, any type of health insurance coverage that is not provided or maintained by a government-run program can be considered a type of commercial insurance.

Most commercial health insurance plans are structured as either a preferred provider organization (PPO) or health maintenance organization (HMO). The main difference between these two types of plans is that an HMO requires patients to use providers and facilities within the network if they want insurance to cover the costs, while a PPO lets patients go outside the network (though their out-of-pocket costs might be greater).

Also, HMOs require patients to choose one primary care physician, who serves as the central provider and coordinates the care that other specialists and healthcare practitioners provide. Referrals from the primary are often necessary to see a specialist.

$31 Billion

The net earnings of the U.S. health insurance industry in 2020, according to the National Association of Insurance Commissioners (NAIC). Profit margins increased 3.8% over 2019.

Types of Commercial Health Insurance Plans

Commercial health insurance can be categorized according to its renewal provisions and the type of medical benefits provided. Commercial policies can be sold individually or as part of a group plan and are offered by public or private companies. Some insurance programs are operated as nonprofit entities, often as an affiliated or regional operation of a larger, for-profit enterprise.

Health insurance in the commercial market is commonly obtained through an employer. Because employers typically cover at least a portion of the premiums, this is often a cost-effective way for employees to obtain health coverage. Employers are often able to get attractive rates and terms because they negotiate contracts with insurers and can offer them a large number of policy customers.

Health insurance provided and/or administered by the government is funded through taxes. It is often reserved for groups, such as seniors (Medicare), low-income patients (Medicaid), and ex-military personnel (Veterans Health Administration programs). Other examples of government-sponsored insurance include the Indian Health Service (IHS), the State Children's Health Insurance Program (SCHIP), and TRICARE.

Self-employed people and small business owners can buy health insurance coverage, but it is often financially beneficial for them to try and join via a group plan through a professional organization or local group.

The specific details of a commercial insurance plan can vary widely and are determined by the company that offers the plan. State regulatory and legislative bodies also dictate certain aspects of what the plans are required to offer and how they must operate. These laws also establish mandates for how and when insurers must pay invoices and reimburse providers and patients, as well as the amount of funds the insurer must keep in reserve to have sufficient capital to pay out benefits.

What Is the Difference Between Commercial and Private Health Insurance?

Technically, there is no difference: Commercial health insurance is provided by private issuers—as opposed to government-sponsored health insurance, which is provided by federal agencies. Commercial insurance may be sponsored by an employer or privately purchased by an individual. Most private insurance providers are for-profit companies, but they can be nonprofit organizations too.

Is Obamacare Commercial Insurance?

Obamacare (a nickname for the Affordable Care Act) is a federal law that is often used to refer to individual health insurance obtained through state health exchanges or marketplaces. These plans are offered by private companies, so technically they are commercial insurance—though they do have to follow some federally mandated guidelines.

What Are Examples of Commercial Health Insurance?

Common types of commercial health insurance include HMOs, PPOs, POS (point-of-service) plans, HRAs (health reimbursement accounts), and LTC (long-term care) plans. Medicare Advantage, Medigap, and other Medicare supplemental plans count as commercial health insurance too. The term can also broaden from general health insurance to include dental.

Qualified Small Employer Health Reimbursement Arrangement (QSEHRA)

What Is a Qualified Small Employer Health Reimbursement Arrangement (QSEHRA)?

A qualified small employer health reimbursement arrangement (QSEHRA), also known as a small business HRA, is a health coverage subsidy plan designed for employees of businesses with fewer than 50 full-time employees. Any money reimbursed is tax-free for employees and tax-deductible by employers.

Key Takeaways

- A QSEHRA is a health cost reimbursement plan that can be offered by small business employers.

- The costs reimbursed are tax-deductible by businesses and tax-free for employees.

- The plan can be used to offset health insurance coverage or repay uncovered medical expenses.

How a Qualified Small Employer Health Reimbursement Arrangement (QSEHRA) Works

A company that decides to offer a QSEHRA agrees to reimburse employees for healthcare-related costs up to a maximum amount each year. Eligible employees may enroll during open enrollment season or after experiencing a qualifying life event, such as a marriage or divorce.

The IRS has released new guidance that allows employers more flexibility for benefit plans during the 2020 economic crisis. Among other things, notice 2020-29 allows employees who initially declined employer-sponsored health coverage an opportunity to enroll in, switch, or drop health coverage or employer-sponsored health coverage. However, these provisions are entirely at the discretion of the employer. If you are not sure about your options, check with your HR or benefits person.

Reimbursements can be used to pay the premiums for health insurance purchased on the market and to pay for qualified medical expenses, including copayments for doctor's office visits, prescriptions, and lab work. Employers may narrow the list of eligible expenses but not expand it and employees must provide proof of their actual medical costs to receive reimbursement.

Employees must have qualified health coverage to use their QSEHRA.

In the 2021 tax year, a company with a QSEHRA may reimburse single employees up to $5,300 per year and employees with families up to $10,700 per year. These figures represent an increase from the 2020 tax year maximums of $5,250 for individual coverage and $10,650 for family coverage.

The limits are set by the Internal Revenue Service (IRS) because the employer is eligible to take a business tax deduction for its costs and the benefit to employees is tax-free.

Employees not covered by a QSEHRA for a full year (e.g., mid-year hires) receive a prorated amount of the full-year maximum reimbursement sum.

History of the Qualified Small Employer Health Reimbursement Arrangement (QSEHRA)

Former President Barack Obama signed the QSEHRA into law on Dec. 13, 2016, as part of the 21st Century Cures Act, and the plans became available to employees on March 13, 2017.

The act corrected a problem for small businesses offering health reimbursement arrangements (HRAs) between 2014 and 2016. During this period, small businesses could be hit with penalties of $100 per employee per day for being out of compliance with the requirements of the Affordable Care Act (ACA).

Qualified Small Employer Health Reimbursement Arrangement (QSEHRA) Eligibility

To qualify to use a QSEHRA, a business must have fewer than 50 full-time employees, provide the QSEHRA on the same terms to all full-time workers, and not have a group health plan or a flexible spending arrangement (FSA)—A QSEHRA is not a group health plan.

Medium and large companies may offer HRAs only as an option alongside group health insurance coverage such as a preferred provider organization (PPO) or health maintenance organization (HMO) plan. Sole proprietors, partners in partnerships, and self-employed employers are not eligible for HMO and PPO plans.

Qualified Small Employer Health Reimbursement Arrangement (QSEHRA) Compliance

To comply with the law, all employees covered by a QSEHRA must benefit from it equally. Employer contributions to each employee's account must be equal.

Employers are not required to include new, part-time, or seasonal workers in the benefits they provide. However, if they offer a QSEHRA to full-time employees, they must cover all of them. Because the ACA governs these arrangements, participating employees must provide proof that they carry the minimum essential health coverage required by the ACA.

QSEHRA plans also receive oversight from the Employee Retirement Income Security Act (ERISA). Following ERISA regulation means employers must give employees a summary plan description that describes their plan benefits.

Finally, should an employer make another form of group health insurance available, they are no longer permitted to offer a QSEHRA plan.

5 Ways for Small Business Owners to Reduce Their Taxable Income

Taxes can be stressful for a small business owner. You wear many hats, and the last thing you want to do is give more of your hard-earned business income to the government. Thankfully, there are many tax savings strategies to reduce your taxable liability as a business owner. If you need ways to reduce your taxable income this year, consider some of the following methods below.

Employ a Family Member

One of the best ways to reduce taxes for your small business is by hiring a family member. The Internal Revenue Service (IRS) allows for a variety of options, all with the potential benefit of sheltering income from taxes. You can even hire your children.

According to Scott Goble, a certified public accountant (CPA) and founder of Sound Accounting, by hiring family members, "small business owners are able to pay a lower marginal rate or eliminate the tax on the income paid to their children."

For example, sole proprietorships do not need to pay social security and Medicare taxes on the wages of a child, nor the Federal Unemployment Tax Act (FUTA) tax. It is important to point out that earnings need to come from justifiable business purposes. The IRS also allows small business owners the benefit of reducing their taxes by hiring a spouse, who would not be subject to the FUTA tax. Depending on the benefits they may have through another job, you may also be able to put aside retirement savings for them.

Start a Retirement Plan

As a small business owner, you give up a 401(k)-match matched by an employer. However, there are several retirement account options that maximize retirement savings and reap valuable tax benefits. For example, with the one-participant 401(k) plan, the IRS allows you to put away up to $57,000 in total contributions for retirement. Some of those retirement planning vehicles include:

- Simplified Employee Pension Plan (SEP)

- IRA or a Roth IRA

- 403(b) plans

There are a variety of different retirement plan options for business owners on the IRS website as a tax savings strategy.

Save Money for Healthcare Needs

One of the best ways to reduce small business taxes is by putting aside money for healthcare needs. Medical costs continue to increase, and while you may be healthy now, saving money for unexpected or future healthcare needs is essential. You can accomplish this through a Health Savings Account (HSA) if you have an eligible high-deductible health plan.

"I also encourage every business owner to explore utilizing an HSA. As medical costs rise, many businesses look to lower the costs of health insurance," says Sean Moore, CFP, ChFC of Smart College Funding. "By utilizing HSAs, the business and the employees can reduce taxes and potentially associated medical costs."

Moore explains that the savings come in three keyways, otherwise known as the triple tax advantage: your contributions are pre-tax, they grow tax-free, and withdrawals for qualified medical expenses are tax-free.

Change Your Business Structure

As a small business owner, you do not have the benefit of an employer paying a portion of your taxes. You are on the hook for the entire amount of Social Security and Medicare taxes. If your business is taxed as a Limited Liability Company (LLC), you still must pay those taxes, though in certain circumstances you may be able to eliminate the employer-half of those two tax responsibilities. This might be a wise switch for some small businesses. While there are many things to consider in this switch, such as paying yourself a reasonable salary and other associated risks, it can be a safe way to reduce your taxable responsibility.

Deduct Travel Expenses

If you travel a lot, you may be able to reduce your business taxes. Business travel is fully deductible, though personal travel does not enjoy the same benefit. However, to maximize your business travel, small business owners can combine personal travel with a justifiable business purpose. Any frequent flier miles earned from business travel can also be redeemed for personal travel later.

The Bottom Line

With wise planning, you can reduce your taxable income as a small business owner and keep more of your money working for you. Just remember to consult a tax professional to make sure you qualify for the potential savings discussed here.

How Becoming an LLC Could Save Taxes Under Trump's Tax Cuts and Jobs Act of 2017

Former President Trump's tax plan—otherwise known as the Tax Cuts and Jobs Act—was signed into law on Dec. 22, 2017. The plan emphasized cutting the corporate tax rate and simplifying the individual income tax system. Whether a hugely profitable multinational corporation or a sole proprietorship, every business that counts as a C corporation (or C-Corp) is now taxed at a flat rate of 21%, down from the original 35%.

One commonly voiced concern was that this new system created a tax loophole that encourages individuals to register as pass-through entities, such as limited liability companies (LLCs) and S Corporations (or S-Corps). Doing so allows their business income to be taxed based on their individual tax rate. This means that the LLC tax rate varies.

What Is a Pass-Through Entity?

An LLC is considered a pass-through entity—also called a flow-through entity—which means it pays taxes through an individual income tax code rather than through a corporate tax code. In addition to LLCs, sole proprietorships, S Corporations, and partnerships are all pass-through businesses. C Corporations are not.

How the LLC Tax Rate Is Calculated

C-Corps tax the profits of owners twice: once at the corporate level and again at the personal level. Not surprisingly, smaller companies not requiring the unique ownership structure of a C-Corp—or the ability to sell shares to the public— most often organize as LLCs or S Corporations.

Meanwhile, because LLC owners can deduct up to 20% of their business income before their tax is calculated, it can be highly beneficial to file as an LLC based on an individual's own personal income tax rate. This could range from 10% to 37% based on everyone's unique filing status and income level.

Small operations that have no plan of raising money from public shareholders but want a higher level of legal and financial protection for their personal assets often form LLCs. All 50 states allow LLCs to consist of just one person. Almost any line of business may be incorporated as an LLC except banking, trust, and insurance businesses. Some states impose additional restrictions, such as California's prohibition against architects, licensed healthcare workers, and accountants registering as LLCs.

How to File as an LLC

Forming an LLC is simple. While it varies by state, the process typically entails filing articles of organization with the state, completing a fill-in-the-blank form, and paying a filing fee. For better financial and legal protection, owners should create an LLC operating agreement even in states that do not require one.

Anyone can form an LLC, but that does not mean anyone can generate income as an LLC. According to CPA Aaron Lesher of Hurdlr, a small business finance app, "a regular salaried employee could theoretically quit their job, create an LLC, and sell their freelance services back to their company to avoid paying a higher income tax rate." However, Lesher notes, "The employee-as-an-LLC idea is a massive audit red flag."

It is not simply up to employers or employees to decide how workers are classified. Their classification depends on how they measure up to various guidelines in the tax code.

"The IRS is very clear on the difference between a contractor and an employee," says Josh Zimmelman, president of Westwood Tax & Consulting LLC, a New York City-based accounting firm. "There are three main factors they look at: financial control, behavioral control, and relationship type."

- Financial control: The IRS looks at whether the worker is paid a regular wage, an hourly rate, or a flat fee per project.[3] "An employee is generally guaranteed a regular wage amount for an hourly, weekly, or another period," the IRS states on its website. "This usually indicates that a worker is an employee, even when the wage or salary is supplemented by a commission. An independent contractor is paid a flat fee for the job. However, it is common in some professions, such as law, to pay independent contractors hourly."

- Behavioral control: The IRS looks at whether a worker has control over when, where, and how they perform the work.[4] "For example, an employee has regular hours and is told where to work; a contractor is offered more freedom as long as the work gets done," Zimmelman says.

- Relationship type: The IRS reviews any written agreements between worker and employer, including the permanency of the relationship.[5] "For example, if a worker receives benefits [such as] health insurance, sick pay, vacation pay, etc., then they are likely an employee," Zimmelman says. "Misclassifying an employee as a contractor may result in penalties, especially if that worker is paid in the same manner as regular employees."

The first step in any plan to turn salaried personal income into LLC income is that the employer must agree to pay the employee as an independent contractor. Certain employers may be game as such an agreement would no longer obligate them to provide health benefits to that worker. However, it is unlikely most employers would participate in such a plan.

"Most employers know that hiring a self-employed person who is considered a disregarded entity—in this case, the LLC—will cause huge problems with the State Department of Labor, and no one wants that," says Abby Eisenkraft, author of 101 Ways to Stay Off the IRS Radar and CEO of Choice Tax Solutions Inc. in New York City.

"If a company tries to represent that a person whose work hours they are controlling—and whose desk space and equipment they are providing—is a contractor, they are inviting the IRS, the state, and the Department of Labor to audit them. And they will not win," she concludes.

Assuming the worker and employer could work out a true independent contractor relationship that would survive an audit, the worker must weigh whether their new pay rate as a contractor combined with the loss of benefits—which might include health, dental, life, and disability insurance, 401(k) contributions, and paid time of—would be worth the tax savings.

So, Do LLCs Save Under the LLC Tax Reform Plan?

Unlike C corporations, LLCs are not considered separate entities, so they do not pay taxes themselves. By default, single-owner LLCs are taxed as sole proprietorships, but LLCs can choose to be taxed as S-Corps or C-Corps, which may benefit some businesses by reducing their employment taxes (Medicare and Social Security taxes).

Let us assume that an LLC wants to be taxed as an S-Corp to save money on payroll taxes while avoiding the double taxation of a C-Corp. Under Trump's plan, the change in business tax rates and the large discrepancy between the flat business tax rate of 21% and the income tax rates between 10-37% might appear to offer tax relief. Tax experts, however, say it is not that simple.

Independent contractors running small corporations cannot easily abuse the system because the terms of the 2017 tax law require that they be employees of their own corporations and pay taxes via payroll. Eisenkraft explains, "In this case, the sole officer will receive a W-2 and be paying taxes at their ordinary tax rate based on wages and other income items on the tax return."

Those wages, in other words, are taxed at the personal rate under the Tax Cuts and Jobs Act of 10%, 25%, or 35%, and subject to Social Security and Medicare taxes (FICA).

"The flow-through portion may be taxed at a reduced rate, but the IRS will not allow that employee to take less than a reasonable salary," Eisenkraft says. "There are many court cases out there where an officer making hundreds of thousands of dollars tries to take a $25,000 salary, and they lose in tax court."

Taxation of Owner's Salary vs. Pass-Through Profits

The tax rate an independent contractor pays on their income is the same under the Trump tax plan as it was under previous tax law, says financial advisor Bradford Daniel Creger, president & CEO of Total Financial Resource Group in Glendale, Calif.

"An individual must pay income taxes on income received from their own efforts—that is, their own earnings—as ordinary income," he says, "Merely forming an entity doesn't change this. It only complicates the returns, but the income tax outcome is the same."

There is one sense in which the Trump tax plan is exploitable, Creger says, "The S corporation."

The simplest and most prevalent example of a pass-through business, the S Corporation currently allows owners to take both salary income and additional income representing the business's profits as an S Corp distribution.

The difference between these two types of income is that the salary is subject to payroll taxes and the S-Corp distribution is not, Creger explains. By separating salary from business profits, the owner saves a slight amount in taxes by avoiding payroll taxes on the amount received as an S-Corp distribution.

But the S-Corp distribution business owners receive is taxed at normal, ordinary income tax rates according to their individual income tax bracket. The only savings from this tax strategy under the current system is the payroll tax savings, Creger says.

Under Trump's tax plan, however, the S-Corp distribution is taxed at 15% instead of at the individual's ordinary rate.[6] Thus, the more owners can receive as a distribution of profits from their businesses, the more they are likely to save.

The Bottom Line

The extent to which business owners have exploited the revised tax code remains to be seen. The Tax Cuts and Jobs Act heavily favors entrepreneurs over salaried workers who earn the same level of income.

Top 10 Home Business Tax Tips

It is said so often that it has become a bit of a cliché, but one of the great virtues of starting a home business are the tax breaks you can claim. Another widely held belief surrounding home businesses, however, is that claiming aggressive—and slightly exaggerated—write-offs are a sure-fire way to attract IRS auditors. In this article, we'll look at some of the more popular home business write-offs as well as some tips on how you can legitimately claim them.

1. Keep a Business Journal

Being audited is not the end of the world. However, being audited and not having the records to back up your deductions can be a nightmare. The simplest way to avoid this unpleasant situation is to keep a daily log of your home business activities. Did you buy paper for the printer in your office? Write it down and either attach the receipt to the page in the case of a hardcopy or scan the receipt in if you are keeping a digital log. The same goes for mileage, phone calls and other costs, as well as payments received by your business.

The more detailed your accounts are, the easier it will be to face an audit. Compiling your daily reports into a monthly tracking sheet will drastically shorten the time it takes you to get your taxes together, and it will have the added benefit of providing a snapshot of your business month-to-month.

2. Write-Off Your Workspace

Writing off a home office can be particularly attractive if you have a line of work that can be neatly confined to a dedicated room. You can still write off part of a shared room, but in either case, space is calculated as a percentage of the total house or apartment area. That percentage is applied to all the related costs, including utilities, insurance, rent or mortgage payments and so on. Do not claim unrelated expense like the installation of a bird fountain in the backyard—those types of stretches make IRS auditors a little testy.

3. Update Your Equipment

Office furniture, software, computers, and other equipment are all 100% deductible within the year that the cost is incurred—you don't need to depreciate. There is an upper limit, and the purchases must be majority-usage (primarily used) and necessary or helpful for business. Within those generous guidelines, however, you should have no problem keeping current. However, a widescreen TV and La-Z-Boy for the office is going to be a hard sell.

4. Save for Retirement

If you are working solely for your home business, you will have to pay the employer's share of Social Security and insurance, but you can deduct half the amount of Social Security and the total premiums for you and any employees (more on that later).

You can also fund retirement plans designed for the self-employed—SEP-IRA, Keogh plans, etc.—and write the contributions off against your personal income tax.

5. Talk Up a Storm

If chatting with clients is a necessary (or helpful) part of your business, it may be worth getting a second phone line or a dedicated business cell phone, as both are 100% deductible. If you only converse with clients occasionally, you can still write off the costs by noting the dates, times and reasons for the calls and then circling the items on your regular phone bill to deduct at tax time.

6. Get Connected

Like the phone bill, you can deduct part of the cost of your internet if you use it for business. There is no absolute percentage to use, but it will be difficult to write off more than 50% if other members of your family are using it for non-business purposes. Be reasonable and pick a defensible percentage that you will not regret in the case of an audit.

7. Entertain Us

You can wine and dine clients—emphasis on clients (preferably paying or likely to pay clients)—and get a tax break. The tendency for business owners at all levels to abuse this write-off has scared many home business owners away from claiming it. However, it is acceptable for you to take out a client for a meal and some entertainment. It will be easier to defend a $200 deduction for a client who has brought you a lot of business than the same meal for a buddy who paid you $20 for an hour's work over the entire fiscal year.

8. Take a Trip, Not a Vacation

Must hit the road to expand your market? Save your receipts. On business trips, your travel expenses are 100% deductible. Although food expenses were deductible at only 50%, Congress made temporary provisions in the Consolidated Appropriations Act, which was signed into law by President Donald Trump in December 2020. The bill allows business meals to be fully deducted if they are paid for or are incurred before Dec. 31, 2022.

Keep all your receipts because even things like dry cleaning and tips are considered a necessary expense when you are out walking the streets in new markets.

Your local day-to-day mileage incurred for business purposes can be written off as well, so give the same attention to tracking your mileage on smaller trips that you would to the expenses of an overnight trip. For many people, the mileage deduction is the more realistic deduction than first-class tickets to New York. Remember, you must be able to justify any trip and preferably show the payoff to your business resulting from it.

9. Employ (Not Just Pay) Your Family

You can use family members as employees and deduct their salaries if you can account for their work and pay the going rate. If you have a business that lends itself to having a spouse and kids help, then use that labor pool. You will pay less than market rates for the help, and you can deduct insurance premiums for them as well.

As a bonus, children under the age of 17 don't incur the Social Security tax, but they can still make contributions to a Roth IRA—so you can teach them a work ethic and saving habits in one go.

10. Make Justifiable Deductions

The most important tip has been a theme throughout, but it is worth repeating just because you have a home business does not mean you can go crazy with deductions. If you don't think you can face down an auditor with detailed proofs justifying the deduction, then perhaps it isn't a deduction you should be taking.

The Bottom Line

A home business can be a rewarding experience, both for the extra income, it can bring in and the tax breaks it yields. A complete read the IRS small business publications is well worth your time. You will learn more about the deductions mentioned here and what conditions need to be met to claim them.

Although it is important to keep accurate records and stick to deductions you can justify, it is also in your interest to maximize your deductions as much as you can while staying within the rules. The IRS guides are not as difficult as they are made out to be, but if you still feel adrift after reading them, then finding a good business accountant will save you time and hopefully a lot of money.

Small Business Tax Obligations: Payroll Taxes

One of the issues small-business owners must contend with is staying current with the many obligations for local, state, and federal taxes. While most business owners hire an accountant or a tax professional to deal with tax-related issues, understanding the tax system is important to those who bear the ultimate responsibility for fulfilling all tax obligations. This article will focus on the business owner's obligations about payroll taxes.

Payroll Tax Obligations

Any business with employees is required to withhold payroll taxes from employees' paychecks and to pay applicable federal, state, and local taxes. The taxes usually withheld from employee paychecks include FICA (Medicare and Social Security taxes) and federal, state, and local income taxes, if applicable.

Other withholding obligations include FUTA (Federal Unemployment Tax Act) and, in states such as California, Hawaii, New Jersey, New York, and Rhode Island, disability insurance taxes. Failure to pay taxes or missing a payment may result in heavy fines and penalties, so it is important to calculate the amount of payroll taxes owed and to pay them on time.

If the small-business owner does not have outside employees but is incorporated, the above rules apply for the owner's paychecks as well, because they are the sole employee of the corporation. If the business is not incorporated and there are no employees, the owner will need to pay estimated taxes on self-employment income each quarter.

Calculating Payroll Taxes

There are three steps to calculating payroll taxes:

1. Determine taxable workers

2. Determine taxable wages

3. Calculate withholding amounts

Taxable Workers

Workers can be employees or independent contractors. Employees are treated as taxable workers subject to payroll taxes, while independent contractors are responsible for paying their own taxes. Usually, workers are considered employees if you have the right to direct and control the way they do their work, rather than merely the results of the work.

However, the lines between independent contractors and employees are not always clear-cut. To help business owners, determine which workers are taxable employees, the Internal Revenue Service (IRS) has common law rules, which include behavioral, financial and relationship tests:

Behavioral Test

A worker is an employee when the employer has the right to direct and control the worker. The employer does not have to direct or control the worker but has the right to do so.

Financial Test

This test looks at the degree of control an employer has over financial aspects of the job. In some professions, having significant control over supplies used for work supports a worker's status as an independent contractor.

One definite way to distinguish an independent contractor from an employee is by the availability of services. An independent contractor is not tied to one company and can advertise services; an employee cannot advertise services unless they are working outside the company as an independent contractor.

Relationship Test

This test refers to the way the employer and the worker perceive their relationship. If an employer-worker relationship is expected to last until the end of a specific project or for a specified period, then the worker is an independent contractor. On the other hand, if the relationship has no or boundaries, the worker is a taxable employee.

Taxable Wages

Taxable wages are compensation for services performed and may include salary, bonuses, or gifts. Some forms of compensation, such as business-expense reimbursements for travel or meals, do not qualify as taxable wages. For the expenses to be nontaxable, employees must verify them through receipts or expense reports. They must also be necessary, reasonable, and business-related.

Calculating Withholding

After you've figured out which workers qualify as taxable employees and which wages are taxable wages, the next step is figuring out the amount you must withhold for federal, state, and local taxes, as well as FICA and FUTA.

Federal Taxes

Every paycheck must withhold federal income taxes for the applicable period. The IRS has two sets of tax tables that employers can use to calculate withholding amounts: the wage bracket tables and the percentage tables.

The wage bracket tables are segregated for five different payroll periods (daily, weekly, bi-weekly, semi-monthly, and monthly). To determine withholding amounts, employers pick the applicable pay period and wage bracket for employees, then read across the table to the column that shows the number of claimed exemptions.

The percentage tables are available for eight payroll periods (daily, weekly, bi-weekly, semi-monthly, monthly, quarterly, semi-annually, and annually) and segregated by marital status. Employers start by reducing wages by the value of exemptions claimed. Next, they use the table corresponding to the employee's marital status and look for the withholding amount based on the wage bracket.

As a business owner, it is your responsibility to look at the two sets of tables and determine which one is appropriate for your business. The percentage tables are more inclusive, in terms of payroll periods, so if you are in a situation where different employees are paid at different payroll periods, then the percentage table should be the table of choice. For example, if your employees are paid quarterly, the percentage tables will be more appropriate than the wage bracket tables. To get these tables, call the IRS or go to http://www.irs.gov/ and ask for Publications 15 and 15-A.

State Taxes

Most states use tables like federal tax tables, and you can get them by going to the tax section of your state's website or contacting the Small Business Administration. You do not need to withhold state taxes in jurisdictions that do not impose state taxes on income, such as Alaska, Florida, Texas, Wyoming, and Washington. Other exceptions include states whose personal income taxes are a fixed percentage of the federal tax, like Arizona, and where state taxes are a fixed percentage of gross wages, such as Pennsylvania.

FICA

The Federal Insurance Contributions Act (FICA) is a federal law that requires employers to withhold Social Security and Medicare taxes from wages paid to employees. It also requires the employer and employee each to pay half of the FICA tax.

Social Security and Medicare taxes are imposed on both the employee at a flat rate of 6.2% for social security and 1.45% for Medicare and the employer 's single flat rate of 6.2% and 1.45%, respectively, creating a combined FICA tax rate of 15.3% (12.4% for Social Security and 2.9% for Medicare). Self-employed individuals are responsible for paying the entire 15.3% tax themselves.

Unlike federal and state taxes, FICA taxes are unaffected by the number of withholding exemptions claimed by the employee. You simply multiply an employee's gross wage payment by the applicable tax rate to determine how much you must withhold and how much you must pay as the employer.

In 2021, the Social Security tax only applies to the first $142,800 of income, also called the Social Security wage base. The wage base is adjusted every year for inflation. The Medicare tax does not have an income limit.

FUTA

Unemployment taxes, or FUTA, are taxes paid solely by the employer. You must pay unemployment taxes if either of the following apply:

a) You pay wages totaling at least $1,500 in a quarter
b) You have at least one employee on any given day for 20 weeks in a calendar year, regardless of whether the weeks are consecutive

The FUTA tax rate is 6.0% for 2020, and it is imposed on the first $7,000 of wages for each employee. However, you can claim credits against your gross FUTA tax to reflect state unemployment taxes that you pay. If you pay your state unemployment taxes when they are due, you are allowed to claim a 5.4% credit, which effectively reduces your FUTA tax rate to 0.6%.

Bringing It All Together

Calculating payroll taxes can be extremely complicated, and it is important to send out payments on time to avoid penalties and late fees. Federal tax payments may be made either online through the Electronic Federal Tax Payment System (EFTPS), or through banks authorized to accept federal payments. If you use the latter method, each payment should be accompanied by Form 8109, which can be obtained by calling the IRS at 1-800-829-4933 or from the IRS website.

FUTA taxes are usually paid quarterly, and income and FICA taxes are deposited semi-monthly or monthly. The IRS usually sends business owners a notice at the end of each year detailing which method to use for the upcoming year.

In general, the timeliness of a deposit is determined by the date it is received. However, a mailed deposit received after the due date will be considered timely if you can establish that it was mailed at least two days before the due date. To learn more about small-business employers' payroll duties, go to http://www.irs.gov/ or call the IRS live help line for businesses at 1-800-829-4933.

The Small Business Health Care Tax Credit

What it is and how to access it

Here is what you need to know about the tax credit that can help owners of small businesses offset the cost of providing health insurance to their employees. It is also available to small tax-exempt organizations.

As a small business owner, you have many decisions to make regarding employee rewards and benefits. Offering the right kind of benefits may entice experienced individuals to apply for open positions. It can encourage current employees to stay with the company longer than they would otherwise.

One of the most important employee benefits to consider is health insurance and this tax credit can help you do it if your business or organization qualifies.

Key Takeaways

- Your business may qualify for the small business health care tax credit if you have fewer than 25 employees, pay average wages less than $50,000 per employee, offer a qualified health plan through the SHOP Marketplace, and pay at least 50% of the cost of employee-only health plans.

- Eligible small businesses may carry the credit backward or forward.

- Eligible small tax-exempt organizations may claim a refundable credit.

What Is the Small Business Health Care Tax Credit?

Certain provisions of the Affordable Care Act (ACA) apply only to small businesses. For example, special insurance options are available only to employers of fewer than 50 employees through the Small Business Health Options Program (SHOP).1

The small business health care tax credit is another feature of the ACA, but it is limited to employers of fewer than 25 employees. It is a sliding-scale credit that is based on the size of the employer. The larger the employer, the smaller the tax credit and vice versa. The maximum credit is 50% of premiums paid for small business employers or 35% of premiums paid for small tax-exempt employers.

The small business health care tax credit is available to eligible businesses for two consecutive tax years. If you have an eligible small business, and your business does not owe tax during any one year, the credit can be carried back or forward to other tax years. The excess amount you paid for employer health insurance premiums over the allowable credit can be claimed as a business expense deduction.

To claim the tax credit, you need to fill out Internal Revenue Service (IRS) Form 8941.

Who Qualifies for the Small Business Health Care Tax Credit?

According to the IRS, an employer with fewer than 25 full-time-equivalent (FTE) employees qualifies for the small business health care tax credit so long as it does all the following three things:

- Pays average wages of less than $50,000 per year for each FTE employee (indexed annually for inflation starting in 2014)

- Offers a qualified health plan to its employees through the SHOP Marketplace (there are rare exceptions to this rule)

- Pays at least 50% of the cost of the employee-only option for each employee.

The employer does not have to cover 50% of the dependent or family health insurance options to qualify.

As mentioned above, the credit works on a sliding scale based on the size of the employer. If you have more than 10 FTE employees, or if your average wage is more than $25,000 (also indexed annually for inflation), the maximum allowed credit will be reduced.

Tax-exempt organizations are also eligible for the tax credit. If you have a tax-exempt business, the credit is refundable to the extent that it does not exceed your income tax withholding and Medicare tax liability. Refunds to tax-exempt organizations are subject to sequestration, which means the refundable amount will be reduced by the current fiscal year sequestration rate.

How to Calculate the Small Business Health Care Tax Credit

Calculating FTEs

For the tax credit, one FTE employee equals 2,080 hours per year. This contrasts with other provisions in the ACA that consider 30 hours per week to be one FTE employee. Any number of part-time employees that adds up to 2,080 hours per year is equivalent to one FTE employee.

Exclude from the calculation of FTE employees any hours worked by any one employee over 2,080 hours per year. Any seasonal employees who worked fewer than 120 days per year should also be excluded from the calculation. However, the health insurance premiums paid by the employer for seasonal workers may still be included in the calculation of the credit amount.

The following should also be excluded from the calculation of FTE employees, and any premiums paid for these individuals should be excluded from the calculation of the credit amount:

- Owner of a sole proprietorship

- Partner in a partnership

- Shareholder of an S Corporation owning more than 2%

- Owner of more than 5% of the business

- Family members of the above

Calculating Average Annual Wages

The total annual wages you pay to all your eligible employees is divided by your total FTE employees to arrive at your average annual wage. For example, if you paid a total of $240,000 to your 10 FTE employees, you divide $240,000 by 10 to arrive at a $24,000 average annual wage.

Limit on Premiums

When calculating the small business health care tax credit, the employer-paid premiums are limited to the premium payment that would have been made if the employer had paid the average premium for the small group market in the rating area.

In other words, the tax credit is limited to the lesser of the actual premiums paid by the employer or the average premium that would have been paid for the small group market in the rating area in which the employee enrolls for coverage.

The average premium table for a given area is published by the Department of Health and Human Services annually.

Let us assume an employer has 10 total employees. The employer covers 50% of all employee-only and family options. Five employees are on an employee-only plan, and each one has a total premium of $4,000. Five employees are on a family plan, and each one has a total premium of $10,000. The total premiums paid were equal to $70,000 ((5 x $4,000) + (5 x $10,000)).

Half of that was paid by the employer, so it paid $35,000 ($70,000 x 50%) in premiums on behalf of its employees. According to the DHHS table, the average premium in the employer's small group market was $6,000 for employee-only plans and $12,000 for family plans. Because the employer paid less than average for its area, it can use the full amount of premiums paid on behalf of employees in the calculation of the tax credit.

The Bottom Line

Health insurance is a benefit that some small business owners think is beyond their economic grasp, even though it is attractive to both prospective and current employees. Governmental incentives such as the small business health care tax credit are there to help bridge the gap, allowing more Americans access to decent health care. Take a good look at the tax implications to see if it can help your small business.

Insurance Coverage: A Business Necessity

Small businesses need adequate protection against property damage and liability

Even when cash is scarce, or revenues down, small businesses should not neglect their insurance needs. Businesses that are underinsured or without broad, proper, and adequate coverage are taking needless risks that could lead to serious financial problems or even bankruptcy. In a crisis, a business that has no insurance or is underinsured can be destroyed.

Key Takeaways

- Small business owners need to have broad, adequate insurance and should periodically review and update their coverage as their circumstances change.

- Policies available to small businesses include business owner's, product liability, professional malpractice, and commercial insurance.

- A homeowner's policy can be an important complement to a business owner's policy, but it usually does not cover claims related to a business conducted in the residence.

- Minimum insurance requirements for a business are often imposed by the state where it is located.

Insurance Basics

Insurance policies are contractual agreements between the insurer and the insured. The contract will detail such information as:

- What is insured

- The cost of the insurance

- The conditions under which a claim may be made

- The terms of payment if the claim is honored

Most insurance policies have deductibles—the amount of money that the insured must pay toward a claim before the insurance company pays anything. Usually, the higher the deductible, the lower the premium—or cost of the insurance. Premiums may be paid on a variety of schedules, including annually (the most common), quarterly, or monthly.

Policies will also indicate the period that they will be in force. In most cases, the insurance company, agent, or broker from whom the business owner bought the insurance will alert them when it needs to be renewed. But, just in case, it is worth noting the date on a calendar and renewing by the deadline, so there is no gap in coverage.

Types of Business Insurance Coverage

There are a number of types of insurance that business owners may want to consider. The appropriate choices will depend on the kind of business, its size, and its risks.

Business Owner's Insurance

A business owner insurance policy offers small and midsize companies broad protection against monetary loss. If their property is damaged by fire or flooding, for example, then the insurance company may pay the cost of repairs. It also might cover the owner's legal liability for bodily injury to someone if the business is held accountable.

Exactly what business owner insurance covers will be specified in the policy. An all-risk policy, which covers every eventuality except for specifically cited exclusions, offers more protection than a named perils policy, which only covers the risks that it names.

Among the risks that may be covered in a business owner's policy are:

- Fire

- Flooding (for instance, when a pipe bursts; for natural disasters, you will need to get flood insurance)

- Other sources of property damage

- Theft

- Bodily injury

- Business interruption for specified reasons

Product Liability Insurance

This type of insurance, obtained at additional cost, may be a necessity if you sell a product that has the potential to injure a user. If you sell a product that injures someone—even if you did not design, manufacture, or distribute the product—then you may have legal liability that should be covered.

Commercial Insurance

A commercial insurance policy may be required if your business is larger and more complex than a simple single-owner or partnership retail operation or is a service-oriented business or professional practice. (A professional practice may also require malpractice insurance, which is covered below.)

Businesses that may require a commercial insurance policy include manufacturers, restaurants, and commercial real estate operators. A commercial policy is typically more expensive than a business owner policy because the risks are correspondingly higher and potentially more costly to the insurance company.

Professional Malpractice Insurance

Professions (including those listed below) that give advice and/or provide services may require professional malpractice insurance to protect themselves from substantial liability in the event of a lawsuit.

- Medicine

- Dentistry

- Law

- Accounting

- Advertising

- Financial planning

- Occupational therapy

- Computer analysis

- Journalism

- Psychotherapy

- Real estate

Insurers calculate premiums for malpractice insurance based on actuarial data for risk, dollar damages, and other relevant factors. Prices vary widely depending on the profession, its subspecialties, and the specific services or advice offered. Neurosurgery, for example, is a profession that carries a high premium for malpractice insurance, while a single-owner, private-practice accountancy normally would pay a smaller premium.

Homeowners Insurance

Home-based businesses that are run from a private residence need to have a comprehensive homeowner's policy as a complement to business owner's insurance.

Coverage typically includes:

- Home or private property damage caused by fire or storms

- Medical costs of occupants' injuries caused by fire, storms, wind, and lightning

- Medical and legal expenses of other people accidentally injured in the insured home

- Loss or theft of specified private property, either in or away from the insured home

However, a homeowner's policy does not cover claims related to a business conducted in the residence. For example, if a customer or delivery person is injured on the premises, then any claim arising from that injury would not be covered by the homeowner's policy.

Under certain circumstances, if you have a home-operated business in which risks are minimal, then you can ask to have a low-cost rider or endorsement added to your homeowner's policy to cover damage to your business assets. However, some insurers will not let you cover your business if your customers, employees, or vendors visit your home. Coverage also may not apply to costly equipment or inventory used or stored on the premises, or if hazardous or combustible materials are used or stored there.

Just as it is a mistake to be uninsured or underinsured, being over insured can be a costly waste of money for a business.

The Dollar Amount of Coverage

The dollar amount of coverage for property damage or loss should be consistent with the replacement cost of the properties involved—including your home, if applicable. Liability coverage is more difficult to calculate, so it is useful to consult with a knowledgeable agent or broker, especially one who is familiar with your type of business.

Some states also impose minimum insurance requirements for businesses. Your agent, broker, or state insurance department can provide the details.

The Bottom Line

If you run a business, then you should discuss your insurance needs in detail with a knowledgeable insurance agent or broker, and be completely candid in describing the business, so that whatever coverage you buy will be adequate. Make sure you know what is covered and what is not—and review your coverage periodically as your business evolves. Once you know exactly what kind of policy or policies you need, you can compare prices from different insurance companies and look for the best value.

Business Liability Insurance

What Is Business Liability Insurance?

Business liability insurance protects the commercial interests of companies and business owners if they face formal lawsuits or any third-party claims. Such policies cover any direct financial liabilities incurred, as well as any legal defense expenses. The three main types of business liability insurance are:

- General liability insurance
- Professional liability insurance
- Product liability insurance

Key Takeaways

- Business liability insurance protects the commercial interests of companies and business owners.
- Types of business liability insurance include general liability insurance, professional liability insurance, and product liability insurance.
- This insurance protects the commercial interests of business-owners from penalties they

may face from litigation waged against them while also covering the associated legal costs.

- The cost of coverage is influenced by the type of business being insured as well as its location (companies located in flood-prone regions are likely to pay more).

Understanding Business Liability Insurance

Small business owners put their personal finances at risk in the event of a business-related lawsuit. Partnerships and sole proprietorships are particularly vulnerable to exorbitant expenses and are consequently in the greatest need of this type of insurance coverage. Even under the structure of a limited liability corporation (LLC), an owner may still be exposed to personal risk.

Business liability insurance protects a company's assets and pays for legal obligations, such as medical costs incurred by a customer who gets hurt on store property, as well as any on-the-job injuries sustained by employees. Liability insurance also covers the cost of a company's legal defense, while paying for any settlement offerings or awards a company is mandated to pay as per legal judgments leveled against them. These costs may include compensatory damages, non-monetary losses suffered by the injured party, and punitive damages.

For businesses that rent the commercial real estate property in which they operate, general liability insurance protects against liability from damage they may suffer due to fire, mold, floods, or other physical catastrophes.

Lastly, business liability insurance also covers claims of false or misleading advertising, including libel, slander, and copyright infringement.

Businesses that tend to carry higher risks than traditional liability insurance covers can augment their coverage limits with excess of loss reinsurance or umbrella insurance.

The Cost of Business Liability Insurance

Coverage costs are determined by a business' perceived risk levels. A building contractor who deals with heavy equipment and dangerous machinery such as cranes and forklifts, for example, will pay more for coverage than an accountant who sits safely behind a desk.

Businesses that fall into the lower risk category may want to consider a business owner's policy (BOP), which combines general liability and property insurance at a more cost-effective rate. Any new or additional business liability insurance policies should contain exclusions clauses to avoid duplication of coverage from competing insurance providers, thereby minimizing costs.

Do not Get Sued: 5 Tips to Protect Your Small Business

How to avoid a lawsuit

As a business owner, it is your responsibility to do everything within your means to limit risk and to keep the business running smoothly. But how do you limit the possibility of a lawsuit to ensure business continuity?

No one can control every eventuality, but there are five actions you can take today to protect your company from being sued tomorrow.

Key Takeaways

- As a business owner, it is your responsibility to do everything within your means to limit risk and to keep the business running smoothly.

- It is wise for a small business to have an attorney on retainer.

- Owners and their employees should avoid making libelous public pronouncements or conducting business that might be considered questionable.

- Putting your business into a trust or incorporating it can help protect your personal assets in the event your firm is sued.

- All businesses should obtain appropriate liability insurance and take steps to protect their computer systems from attack.

1. Watch What You Say and Do

The image of your business is critical. That is one reason owners, and their employees should avoid making any public announcements or conducting any business that might be considered questionable. That includes libelous or potentially slanderous statements, but it also means not doing business with unscrupulous individuals. You may not think that working for a group of individuals known for shoddy business practices would be problematic because you know your company's ethics are above reproach, but if they are exposed, your company's name could be linked to them in the fallout.

You and your employees should also try to limit any conflict of interest and avoid situations where one may present itself. Situations such as these can damage your integrity as a business owner and could land you in legal hot water.

Sitting on the town council and helping pass an ordinance that benefits your business, for example, would be a conflict of interest, even if you did not decide with any benefit for your company in mind.

2. Hire a Competent Attorney

When starting up your business, interview attorneys so you have legal counsel on standby. You may need a lawyer to advise you before you take an action—or to recommend the steps to take if you have been sued.

It is a clever idea to retain an attorney who is familiar with the local laws and customs in the area in which the business operates and has expertise in a particular field, if necessary. If your company anticipates legal challenges from the Internal Revenue Service (IRS) or a state department of taxation, it may make sense to hire a tax attorney.

There are several potential resources to help you find a good attorney. Professional references from other business owners can be a helpful avenue to pursue or you can consult professional organizations to which the company belongs (such as the local chamber of commerce or any sector association). Of course, you can always try cold calling (and interviewing) from the phone book.

3. Separate Yourself from Your Business

Many entrepreneurs own and operate their businesses as sole proprietorships. This can be problematic in the event the company is sued because the owner's individual assets (for example, cars or a home) are easy to attack or attach in a court of law.

One way to limit the possibility that an owner's personal assets might be the target of a suit is to have a trust own the business. A trust is a legal entity that, in most cases, files its own tax return and can own property, businesses, cash, securities, and a host of other assets. If a properly established trust owns a business and it is sued, in most cases the only assets that can be attacked or attached in a court of law are those that are in the trust itself.

Incorporating is another means of separating your company's finances from your own. This makes your house and personal wealth safe from attack even in the event you lose your business in a judgment. The downside to incorporating. You must understand and keep up with the additional laws, reports, and taxes that the government requires for a corporation.

4. Insure Yourself

All businesses should obtain liability insurance—just in case, for example, a customer slips and falls in your place of business. Certain professionals, such as insurance agents and consultants, should also consider obtaining errors and omissions insurance (E&O) to ensure their business is protected if a customer or client accuses the owner of making an error or not living up to a contract.

If the business has a formal board of directors, it may also make sense to secure directors and officers (D&O) liability insurance to protect the directors' personal assets in the event of a larger suit against the company.

In addition to purchasing insurance, you can build liability protection into your contracts. If an act of nature, a specific supplier, or some other uncontrollable act could make it impossible for you to fulfill a contract (thus exposing you to legal action), you should include in that contract that you are not liable for incomplete work due to these factors. Discussing with your lawyer the possible clauses and legal phrases you will need in your work contracts can reduce your need for a lawyer later in your business venture.

5. Protect Your Files

Most businesses these days work extensively on computers, which requires emphasizing the safety of your computer system. Businesses need updated antivirus and other types of security software loaded and activated on their systems. If a virus were to bring down a computer system, it could cause a business to be unable to perform certain contracted work. Also, key files could be lost or stolen, which could then lead to legal action from clients and/or suppliers.

Make sure you have a set of backed-up files to refer to in the event of a massive technological breakdown. This could mean performing daily, weekly, or even monthly backups, and making your clients aware of the ones you employ. If you keep these files at your place of business, store them in a fireproof safe. Or store them off-site to ensure your company's continued safety. Should the very worst happen to the rest of your materials and supplies, your backups would be protected.

In the event of a disaster such as a hurricane or fire—or a pandemic, as we have now learned—will your business be able to function? Failure to operate could lead to the company's inability to live up to certain contractual obligations or to satisfy other legal/financial agreements.

Consider securing alternative work sites, portable generators, call trees, and/or ways to have employees work remotely to make it a little easier for your company to perform its work when the forces of nature throw you a curveball.

The Bottom Line

Business owners are responsible for protecting their companies and their personal assets in the event of a lawsuit. With these five actions under your belt, your business should be in a stronger position to avoid legal action—or to confront it and come out unscathed.

The 5 Licenses and Permits You Need for Your Home-Based Business

Find out which ones are required for you to operate legally

Individuals who want to start home-based businesses are often so eager to get underway that they omit a critical step: making sure they have all the requisite licenses and permits to legally operate their new business. This can cause major problems in the future. The last thing you want is to get your business up and successfully running, only to have it suddenly shut down by a government authority because you lack a necessary permit. It is well worth the required time and minor investment to make sure that you have all business licensing squared away right from the start.

Specific licensing, zoning, and permit requirements vary according to locality, so check with the Small Business Administration (SBA) to obtain specific requirements for your state. However, the basic licensing and permit requirements are consistent from one state to another. Here are the five you need to know about.

Key Takeaways

- Before starting a business out of your basement or home office, be sure that all your regulatory boxes have been checked off to operate legally.

- Many types of business require a state-issued license.

- Sometimes professional organizations require a license to practice.

- You may require permits if customers will be frequenting your home; a home business may also need to be set up to pay sales taxes.

1. General Business License

Any type of business, including home-based businesses, must obtain a local city or county business license. This is a basic license to engage in business activities within the local jurisdiction. If your city or county does not have a specific business licensing department, you can obtain information on obtaining a basic business license at your local tax office. The license may be designated as a business tax certificate, reseller's certificate, or license.

In addition to obtaining a general business license, check that your business is following local zoning ordinances. Sometimes this is certified when you apply for your business license, but in other areas, you need to double-check with the city or county zoning department. Neighborhoods, usually in the form of homeowner's associations, also tend to have restrictions on the operation of home businesses. If your business does not meet local zoning ordinances or neighborhood requirements, it is possible to obtain an exception or variance, but go through the proper channels to do so.

2. Professional License

Certain types of home-based businesses, such as daycare centers, hairstyling, legal services, or financial advisor services, require state or federal professional licensing or certification. Contact your state business office or visit the official state website to obtain a list of all occupations or businesses that require professional licensing.

3. Health and Safety Permits

Depending on the type of business you intend to operate, you may need to get an inspection and permit from the local fire department. This is most required if customers or clients come to your home to conduct business. It is not usually required if your home-based business only provides goods or services online unless you keep an inventory of potentially flammable products at your home.

Less commonly required are environmental licenses or health department permits. Such licenses or permits are most required for businesses engaged in the wholesale or retail selling of food and beverage products. In any event, it is easy enough to check with state environmental protection agencies or local health departments to find out if your business requires any type of environmental inspection or permit.

In some jurisdictions, operating a business without a proper sales tax license is a criminal violation.

4. Sign Permit

If you are planning to put out a sign where you live to advertise your business, make certain that you follow all local ordinances. All cities or counties have specific sign ordinances in effect that govern the size, type, and location of business signs. Lighting of signs is also usually restricted. In addition to city or county laws, many homeowners' associations, condominiums, and apartment complexes have their own restrictions on commercial signs. If you own your home, look over your deed and check with your homeowner's association. If you rent, obtain permission from your property owner.

5. Sales Tax License

In some localities, a sales tax license is part of the general business license. However, in other areas, a separate sales tax license is required in addition to a local business license. The local department from which you obtain a business license can tell you if you must obtain a separate sales tax license and where to get it at either the state or local level. Make sure that you have this covered before you open your business.

The 4 Most Common Reasons a Small Business Fails

Running a small business is not for the faint of heart

Running a business is not for the faint of heart; entrepreneurship is inherently risky. Successful business owners must possess the ability to mitigate company-specific risks while simultaneously bringing a product or service to market at a price point that meets consumer demand levels.

While there are a number of small businesses in a broad range of industries that perform well and are continuously profitable, 20% of small businesses fail in the first year, 50% go bankrupt after five years, and only 33% make it to 10 years or longer, according to the Small Business Administration (SBA).

To safeguard a new or established business, it is necessary to understand what can lead to business failure and how each obstacle can be managed or avoided altogether. The most common reasons small businesses fail include a lack of capital or funding, retaining an inadequate management team, a faulty infrastructure or business model, and unsuccessful marketing initiatives.

Key Takeaways

- Running out of money is a small business's biggest risk. Owners often know what funds are needed day to day but are unclear as to how much revenue is being generated, and the disconnect can be disastrous.

- Inexperience managing a business—or an unwillingness to delegate—can negatively impact small businesses, as can a poorly visualized business plan, which can lead to ongoing problems once the firm is operational.

- Poorly planned or executed marketing campaigns, or a lack of adequate marketing and publicity, are among the other issues that drag down small businesses.

1. Financing Hurdles

A primary reason small businesses fail is a lack of funding or working capital. In most instances a business owner is intimately aware of how much money is needed to keep operations running on a day-to-day basis, including funding payroll; paying fixed and varied overhead expenses, such as rent and utilities; and ensuring that outside vendors are paid on time. However, owners of failing companies are less in tune with how much revenue is generated by sales of products or services. This disconnects leads to funding shortfalls that can quickly put a small business out of operation.

A second reason is business owners who miss the mark on pricing products and services. To beat out the competition in highly saturated industries, companies may price a product or service far lower than similar offerings, with the intent to entice new customers. While the strategy is successful in some cases, businesses that end up closing their doors are those that keep the price of a product or service too low for too long. When the costs of production, marketing, and delivery outweigh the revenue generated from recent sales, small businesses have little choice but to close.

Small companies in the startup phase can face challenges in terms of obtaining financing to bring a new product to market, fund an expansion, or pay for ongoing marketing costs. While angel investors, venture capitalists, and conventional bank loans are among the funding sources available to small businesses, not every company has the revenue stream or growth trajectory needed to secure major financing from them. Without an influx of funding for large projects or ongoing working capital needs, small businesses are forced to close their doors.

To help a small business manage common financing hurdles, business owners should first establish a realistic budget for company operations and be willing to provide some capital from their own coffers during the startup or expansion phase. It is imperative to research and secure financing options from multiple outlets before the funding is necessary. When the time comes to obtain funding, business owners should already have a variety of sources they can tap for capital.

67%

The percentage of small businesses that fail within the first 10 years, according to the Small Business Administration.

2. Inadequate Management

Another common reason small businesses fail is a lack of business acumen on the part of the management team or business owner. In some instances, a business owner is the only senior-level person within a company, especially when a business is in its first year or two of operation.

While the owner may have the skills necessary to create and sell a viable product or service, they often lack the attributes of a strong manager and do not have the time to successfully oversee other employees. Without a dedicated management team, a business owner has greater potential to mismanage certain aspects of the business, whether it be finances, hiring, or marketing.

Smart business owners outsource the activities they do not perform well or have little time to successfully carry through. A strong management team is one of the first additions a small business needs to continue operations well into the future. It is important for business owners to feel comfortable with the level of understanding each manager has regarding the business' operations, current and future employees, and products or services.

Lack of a business plan and an unwillingness to adapt the plan as challenges arise can create structural problems for a small company that are insurmountable.

3. Ineffective Business Planning

Small businesses often overlook the importance of effective business planning prior to opening their doors. A sound business plan should include, at a minimum:

- A clear description of the business

- Current and future employee and management needs

- Opportunities and threats within the broader market

- Capital needs, including projected cash flow and various budgets

- Marketing initiatives

- Competitor analysis

Business owners who fail to address the needs of the business through a well-laid-out plan before operations begin are setting up their companies for serious challenges. Similarly, a business that does not regularly review an initial business plan—or one that is not prepared to adapt to changes in the market or industry—meets potentially insurmountable obstacles throughout the course of its lifetime.

To avoid pitfalls associated with business plans, entrepreneurs should have a solid understanding of their industry and competition before starting a company. A company's specific business model and infrastructure should be established long before products or services are offered to customers, and potential revenue streams should be realistically projected well in advance. Creating and maintaining a business plan is key to running a successful company for the long term.

4. Marketing Mishaps

Business owners often fail to prepare for the marketing needs of a company in terms of capital required, prospect reach, and accurate conversion-ratio projections. When companies underestimate the total cost of early marketing campaigns, it can be difficult to secure financing or redirect capital from other business departments to make up for the shortfall. Because marketing is a crucial aspect of any early-stage business, it is necessary for companies to ensure that they have established realistic budgets for current and future marketing needs.

Similarly, having realistic projections in terms of target audience reach and sales conversion ratios is critical to marketing campaign success. Businesses that do not understand these aspects of sound marketing strategies are more likely to fail than companies that take the time to create and implement cost-effective, successful campaigns.

As this book ends, we want to remind you. Read it again, hi-light it, start a small business network, share ideas, and before long, you will be living the dream. The dream is freedom from the sh!t that comes from working from someone else. See you at the bank.

CPSIA information can be obtained
at www.ICGtesting.com
Printed in the USA
BVHW021213210622
640287BV00002B/9